WHY CHRISTIAN MARRIAGES ARE BREAKING UP

by

Gerald L. Dahl

Thomas Nelson Publishers
Nashville

Third printing

Library of Congress Cataloging in Publication Data

Dahl, Gerald L
  Why Christian marriages are breaking up?

  Includes bibliographical references.
  1. Marriage. 2. Divorce. I. Title.
BV835.D33   301.42   78-27693
ISBN 0-8407-5154-0

To Peter, Stephen, and Leah
With Love

Contents

Preface

Throughout the years that I have been counseling marriages, I have come to realize that while I have been teaching each of the couples about marriage, they in turn have been teaching me. Day after day couples pass through my office, each leaving their lesson about relationships and life. In many respects this book is a compilation of that which I have learned. I am deeply grateful to each of my patients for this.

Several years ago one of them gave me a copy of the book *Love Is Now* by Peter E. Gillquist. Little did I know what would follow from the seed that was planted by the gift of that book. I was personally blessed by its message, and in turn began giving it to patients who were seeking the love and peace God offers them.

Through a mutual friend, Ake Lundberg, I had the privilege of meeting the author whose book had been so useful to my counseling practice.

Several months passed. One day while driving to a rural medical clinic where I provide counseling services one day a week, the Lord made it distinctly clear that He wanted me to write a book. Thoughts about relationships began rushing through my head. I came to a more complete realization of all I had learned about marriages during the years I had been counseling couples. Arriving at the clinic a few minutes early, I quickly wrote out a rough chapter outline. I tossed the outline into my briefcase and forgot about it for the rest of the day.

Two days later I received an early morning telephone call from Peter Gillquist. He got right to the point by telling me he thought I should consider writing a book. To his surprise, I told him the Lord had sent that message two days earlier. The timing of these two events was a clear sign to me that it was God's will, and therefore this book is indeed His.

For years we have watched the divorce rate climb. We have felt some degree of security in the midst of this marital turmoil as Christian marriages have stood strong as an affirmation of the permanence and sacredness of the bonds of holy matrimony. But this story is changing. With grave concern we now see how the blight of marital problems has deeply infected Christian marriages as well. The rapidly rising divorce rate shows we are experiencing an unprecedented epidemic of marital failure in the evangelical Christian church.

This book is written to the crucial problem of the failure of Christian marriages. My sincere desire and prayer is that God will speak to each Christian couple who comes to this book looking for answers to their marital problems. And to all who read this book, may you find that abundant joy God intended all married couples to experience through His divine plan of marriage.

To Peter Gillquist I express my sincere gratitude for his generous help in so many different ways throughout the writing of the manuscript. Above all, I appreciate his special attention and support for new authors, which was so necessary for me as I went through my first experience of writing a book.

While preparing this manuscript, I corresponded with several Christian leaders, asking them pointed questions about their problems and for their advice to others going through these same things. Many of their responses are used in the book, and I extend to them my appreciation for their cooperation.

I wish to thank my colleague, Dr. Jon Wempner for his very helpful suggestions in various areas of the book. Thanks also to my good friend and brother in Christ, Harold S. Christensen, whose mind I admired as he offered helpful comments in the review of the manuscript.

Then there is "Mimi," Mrs. Beryl Brown, my dear mother-in-law, who stood by me in a special way during the final stages of the writing. She graciously performed a variety of tasks—from proofreading the text to cooking and caring for the family—while my wife devoted all her time to typing the manuscript.

Finally there is Judy, from whom I received special strength and inspiration to keep writing. Her presence is evident throughout the entire book. She listened to my thoughts. She read and helped revise each chapter. She typed the final manuscript. She allowed me to write openly about our marriage. But above all, she loved and prayed me through the entire event. In many ways, this is really *our* book to you.

Gerald L. Dahl

Golden Valley, Minnesota
September, 1978

1

Once Was Not Enough

A familiar quietness fell over the reception area as the answering service took over the telephone calls and the last patients of the day left from their therapy sessions. The waiting room that had been filled with the emotion and drama of troubled lives was now empty. Office doors were locked and the voices of staff personnel faded in the hallways as they went their separate ways at the close of another day.

The clinic was almost deserted on this late Thursday afternoon except for a few of us who led evening therapy groups. I was one of them. For years in my marriage counseling practice I had devoted this particular evening to group therapy for couples. It had become so routine that everyone in my family knew Thursday night and "Daddy's late night" were synonymous. These evenings were often exhausting, as couples would expose in vivid detail the crises that threatened the very lives of their marriage relationships. Long ago I had learned that relationships, just like individuals, can become critically ill. Certainly the termination of a relationship has some of the same profound effects upon people as does the actual loss of someone through physical death.

I never knew exactly what to expect as my five couples would come together each week for their one-and-a-half-hour session. Sometimes it was warm and caring; other times it was hostile and tense, often requiring an extension of the session to give them some means to continue together until they returned the next Thursday.

Although the sessions varied from week to week, this one was to be unique. Tonight was to be a first for the clinic, and it was to happen in *our* group. Knowing there are few things left to distinguish themselves as "firsts," I had asked several of my colleagues what they felt was "the least likely thing you would expect to happen in couples' group therapy." I received many very interesting responses, but not one of them had been able to guess correctly. What's more, they had not even believed the answer when I told them!

Tonight there was to be a *wedding* in our couples' session—an honest-to-goodness, genuine, bona fide wedding! There would be a license, a minister, a ceremony, and everything else to make the event legal and official. As for me, I was more nervous and excited than if I were the father of the bride.

I realized that my joy and excitement was for more than just the wedding. What could be more thrilling for a marriage counselor than to share in the experience of bringing a couple *back* together to say their vows a second time! We were resurrecting a marriage that had been declared legally dead.

The bride and groom were Donna and Mark, a Christian couple who had been married for twenty-one years.* They had raised two children and had what appeared to be a successful marriage. No one knew they had problems, including Mark. But two years ago Donna had announced

*Mark and Donna's story is true, but their names have been changed. Their permission allows me to share this experience with you.

to him that she was tired of the prison she found herself in and was going to divorce him.

"My needs aren't being met, and I have to find out who I really am," she told him as she presented the divorce papers. At that time she did not consider marriage counseling an option. She moved out, leaving Mark stunned and single.

It took her only a short time to realize she had made a terrible mistake. What she had been looking for was latent—but present—right back in her previous marriage relationship.

She came to Mark, telling him how God had touched her life. Her eyes had been opened to see the priceless treasure she had abandoned by breaking the covenant they had made. She asked his forgiveness, hoping that somewhere in his heart he would have a desire to try again. Donna told Mark she realized her needs could never be met in the same way outside the marriage as they could be with him. She carried a mixture of peace and apprehension within her. She knew now that Jesus Christ was again in control of *her* life, but she was apprehensive as to whether or not Mark could trust her enough to let her back into *his* life.

Mark was still in love; he had never stopped loving Donna. Still numb from the shock of rejection and divorce, he was scared to death to try again. He wanted to shake off his feelings, but they stuck with him like a magnet. Have you ever desperately wanted something but were too frightened to reach out and take the chance of getting hurt again? This is where Mark was when Donna came back to him and said, "I love you and want to live with you for the rest of my life."

Shortly thereafter they came to my office, nervously introduced themselves, and told me their story. They sensed the need for professional help before going any further in repairing their relationship. Mark said, "I have never experienced a pain as severe as when Donna told me she was leaving. I couldn't handle it if it were to happen again." Although understandably frightened, he asked me to help him overcome his fears so he could once again trust his wife. I assured him that his very presence in my office was a beginning of this trust.

Although I said nothing about this at the time, I determined to check out very closely his wife's sincerity in her renewed commitment to him. Nothing is more destructive to a person than repeated rejection. Eventually that person finds it nearly impossible to trust *anyone,* even though the desire and basis for trust may be there.

We accepted them into our group, and they began to attend our sessions. Remarriage was brought up to them from time to time by the other group members, but during those first few sessions it was quickly dropped or sidestepped in favor of a more comfortable subject. Even though they were both interested in remarriage, their insecurity was reflected by the eggshells they walked on whenever the subject came up.

One day nearly six months into our weekly sessions, I received a telephone call from Donna. "Great news!" she said, "Mark and I have talked, and we are ready to get married again." Before I could express my elation over their decision, she continued. "There's more. We want to be married in the Thursday group. We feel closer to these people than anyone else in the world, and we want to share our joy with them."

I listened as Donna emphasized that they wanted it to be a simple ceremony at the end of the regular session, with only our group members in attendance. They were sensitive to the fact that people in the group would still have matters they needed to discuss in therapy. Mark and

Donna wanted them to be sure to have plenty of time for sharing personal needs before the wedding. We set the date!

Tonight was the wedding. Everyone arrived at the usual time to take their places in the circle, carrying on the light conversation that often preceded the session. After a few minutes I walked in, closed the door, loosened my tie, and rolled up my shirt sleeves. These gestures have become a silent signal that the group session is beginning, so the conversation quieted.

My eyes scanned the circle. Everyone looked the same as usual except for Donna, who was sitting beautifully poised in her long dress, and Mark in a new suit and fresh haircut. Anyone would have seen this was a special evening for them. They sat quietly, politely indicating that they preferred just to listen during the first part of our session, knowing their time was to come later.

During the opening moments of the session I usually collect my thoughts and study the facial expressions and other nonverbal messages of the group members as a key to know where to begin. Tonight it was different; they were watching me for the same reason. I expressed my surmounting joy and satisfaction over what was going to happen later in the evening. I explained that we would have group as usual for about an hour, and then we would stop to have the wedding.

With that our session began. Tom talked about the stress he was experiencing in his job and the effect it was having on his marriage. Jan and Larry shared about their very rough week and expressed to the group uncertainty regarding the future of their relationship. Mark, who was usually reluctant to talk, responded with authority, telling them dissolving their marriage would give them far more serious problems than they were facing now. With that,

Donna jumped in with a large dose of warm support and sincere faith that Jan and Larry would find the happiness she and Mark now had. It occurred to me that when they left the group I would miss the tremendous encouragement she consistently gave to the others.

At nine I heard the front door of the reception area open. Doug, an ordained minister who is now in private practice as a marriage counselor, walked down the hallway. We have been friends for years, so I was especially pleased when he had consented to conduct the ceremony. He had worn his long black clergy robe to add dignity to the occasion. I suggested we stop the session to have our wedding.

The group room was quickly transformed into a simple chapel by the rearranging of chairs into rows. Other pieces of furniture were moved, leaving an open area at one end of the room for the wedding party. Meanwhile, Mark and Donna were getting acquainted with Doug in my office across the hall.

Everyone was excited and *overly* helpful. Three men carried one chair that could easily have been moved by any one of them alone. But I was the most excited of all. I caught myself dashing back and forth between the group room and my office, trying to take care of everything for everyone. I kept telling myself, "This cannot be happening—not in group therapy on Thursday night at the clinic." But it was!

As Donna, Mark, and Doug entered, a hush came over the room. Doug looked at me and said, "Jerry, they want you to be best man."

I jumped to my feet with the same enthusiasm I had in high school when the football coach called me off the bench to enter the game. Doug quietly reminded the couple that they needed one more witness for the ceremony. Realizing they had no favorites, Donna extended her hand to Karen, who was usually very shy. However, she confidently stood to her feet and joined the rest of the wedding party.

The group room now possessed the sacredness of a chapel, and I knew the presence of the Lord was there. The warmth of the Holy Spirit graced the room as Doug prayed, inviting God's blessing upon what was about to take place.

I was extremely proud of Doug. In his long robe and with his small black marriage manual, he was ready to begin. I noticed a dignity and authority I had never seen in him before. I realized that my relationship with him was usually as a colleague in marriage counseling. Tonight he was more. He was a minister of the gospel, God's servant with divine authority to conduct this very sacred event.

My reaction to Doug was a personal reminder that marriage is far more than a mere legal event. It is a holy agreement designed by God to be unique and special, existing above all other human relationships. How often I had emphasized to my students at Bethel College that marriage is of divine design, possessing a sacredness unique to that relationship.

The silence was broken as we heard those familiar words:

Dearly beloved, we are gathered together here in the sight of God and in the presence of this company, to join together this man and this woman in holy matrimony.

Marriage is an honorable estate, instituted of God, blessed by our Lord Jesus Christ, and commended by St. Paul to be honorable among all men.[1]

As I listened to the words, they seemed to come at me with special meaning. What was happening in this little group therapy room *was* "in the sight of God . . . and in the presence of this company."

What a company! I thought. Donna and Mark had only known these people for a short time, yet they were closer to them than lifelong friends. These couples identified, shared, and talked openly with each other about the problems of their relationships. I was pleased with all of them for trying to heal their marriages instead of walking away from them in divorce. As I glanced over my shoulder I saw several couples holding hands, and I hoped they too were renewing their vows in their hearts.

With conviction, Doug reminded Mark and Donna that this covenant was not to be entered into lightly or unadvisedly, but reverently, soberly, and in the fear of God. Happily, they did not need much reminding; they were aware of the sacred, permanent commitment they were now reconfirming. Tonight they were saying with sincere, total commitment the vows they had exchanged twenty-three years earlier in their teens.

Now Doug was asking Mark to repeat that section of the vows requiring the "I will." Donna's big blue eyes, filled with love, never left Mark's face.

Eagerly taking her turn, she recited with familiarity the words of her vows. It would hardly have been necessary for Doug to read them first, for they seemed indelibly written in her mind. Then came the key moment. "Do you solemnly promise, before God and these witnesses, that forsaking all others for him alone, you will perform unto him all the duties that a wife owes to her husband, until God, by death, shall separate you?"

There was a moment of silence, not reflecting any hesitation but instead giving the moment the sobriety it deserved. I watched as her eyes, having already said *yes,* took on a special glisten as her voice replied with a confident, loving, "I will."

A broad smile came over Mark's face. His fear and the insecurity of losing his wife were gone for good.

For this couple who had become so special to all of us, *once was not enough*. They had, by God's grace, received a second chance.

The solemn mood of the ceremony quickly lightened as the group moved into the clinic waiting room. It had become the banquet hall for the reception. The table, usually filled with tattered magazines worn from being nervously paged by waiting patients, now hosted a beautiful buffet of food that the newlyweds had insisted on providing. Our clinic had added its part to the evening by providing a three-tiered wedding cake, which was cut to the flash of Polaroid cameras.

The hour grew late but the excitement never diminished. As the couples began leaving, I could sense they were still trying to grasp the fact that they had been to both a group therapy session and a wedding.

Finding myself alone, I walked back into the group room and began to relax. I drained the last cup of coffee from the pot. Sitting with my feet up and lights out, I watched the couples find their way to their cars in the parking lot below. Donna and Mark were last, their arms filled with plates, cups, and the remains of the buffet. The wedding was over and a new marriage had begun. As they drove off I sensed a satisfaction reserved only for marriage counselors at a happy ending.

But all kinds of questions began tumbling through my head. Why are so many Christian marriages falling by the wayside? Why are the marriages of evangelical leaders, pastors, and other spiritual pacesetters breaking up? Why did Mark and Donna's marriage fail the first time? What made Donna want to try again? What happens when Christian marriages fail, and for what reasons are some saved?

My eyes turned back again to the parking lot. I thought about the other couples finding their way to their cars. How many would see no future in staying together and ultimately get a divorce?

Summary

Mark and Donna, by God's grace and their desire to save their relationship, were able to experience the resurrection of their marriage.

For a marriage to be healthy, it is crucial that both partners understand its sacred nature.

2

The Invisible Pain
on the Other Side

"Divorce is emotionally like a massive heart attack that leaves you disabled and in pain."

This was the vivid description Mary gave me as she recounted her own recent divorce. Mary is a nurse at one of our medical centers and is basically a very strong, confident person who is well experienced in her profession. But her divorce struck her down in a way she had never previously experienced, even though her life had known other crises.

Despite the fact that both she and her husband felt that divorce was their best choice, it was extremely painful for her and left her disabled. She missed several months of work, during which time she was hospitalized for psychiatric care of her depression. All this was from the trauma of her divorce.

At one point it was nearly fatal. With a shaky voice she told me how she had sat alone for hours in the middle of the night, staring at the pills that could end her life. Because of her medical background she knew the exact number for a lethal overdose.

There they were, all counted out on the kitchen table awaiting her decision. Through God's protective love she chose to go on living. But when she looked back on the whole experience she told me, ''Never again do I want to experience *that pain*. It was terrible and nothing seemed to make it go away.''

Eventually, Mary started to recover. Today she is doing quite well as a single person, but the painful effects of the divorce will always remain with her. Over one year later she was shopping alone one night at a local shopping center. Making her way through the crowded mall, she suddenly found herself face to face with her ex-husband. As their eyes met they both froze in their tracks. Neither knew just what to do. After a moment that seemed like a century, they passed without speaking.

Mary's wound was opened once again. She ran out of the shopping center with tears streaming down her face. She was so upset that it took her over an hour to find her car in the parking lot. A week off work and a couple of counseling sessions helped start the healing process once again.

''The pain will always be there,'' she said, ''but now I think I have it in a place where it will not interfere as easily with my day-to-day living.''

I asked Mary if she knew why the pain was so intense, especially since the divorce had been her choice as well as her husband's. Her answer included many factors relating to the profound readjustment she was required to make. There was less money and more work. She was now responsible for little things she had previously taken for granted, such as having the car serviced and buying snow tires for winter.

However, one reason seemed to stand out above all the others. When you get a divorce you choose to end your marriage relationship. However, with that choice you also terminate other relationships, that you want and need. In one way or another a divorce affects almost all your relationships, shaking the very foundation of your support system.

In Mary's situation, by divorcing her husband she also lost a set of parents-in-law she had grown to love. Mary had never known her natural father because he died when she was an infant. Therefore, her husband's father had been especially close to her.

Through the marriage Mary had also developed a relationship with a sister-in-law who had become her best friend. They vowed to continue the friendship in spite of the divorce, but after three months they never saw each other any more.

All the couples with whom Mary and her husband had socialized assured her she was still part of the gang. But after a couple of parties where she was the only single person there, the invitations and contacts stopped.

Mary's story is just one of many. The painful experience is the same; only the people are different. Please hear me when I tell you that a large part of the pain of divorce comes from the fact that with the *voluntary termination* of the marriage, many other relationships are *terminated involuntarily.* Your old support system is gone. A new one must be built. But in the interim, you are alone.

Divorce is not a solution, but rather an exchange of problems. You give up one set of frustrations only to take on another. You may walk away from your marital problems, but you take on others that are just as bad, if not worse. No matter who you are or what the circumstances of your marriage, you will experience in divorce a whole new set of emotional and social upheavals in your life that you never dreamed were possible.

Listen to the plea of the former wife of a missionary who worked in the home office of a well-known evangelical outreach agency, as we discussed counsel she would give to Christians with marriage difficulties: "If they are considering divorce as an option, I'd like to shout, scream, stomp, and yell that it's not the best way out. Even if they see it as a moral option, the grass on the other side is not necessarily greener, and sometimes only brown and dry."

The overwhelming majority of couples choose divorce far too quickly as a "solution" to their marriage problems, only to awaken in total disillusionment over their new single status. Locally in the Twin Cities area, social workers in our divorce courts prepare people for the reality of divorce by acquainting them with the five phases of loss experienced in death as outlined by Elisabeth Kübler-Ross: *denial, depression, anger, bargaining,* and *a form of acceptance,* in that order.[1]

I believe it is a very accurate comparison to equate divorce with death as far as the emotional experience is concerned.

Divorce is not a solution. Only now, after my years of exposure to the pain known by those going through divorce, do I begin to understand God's powerful response: "For I *hate* divorce, says the Lord the God of Israel [italics mine]."[2]

Even we who know Christ and seek to follow Him have been bought off by a comfort-loving society in which many people see marriage as a temporary state to be honored "as long as we both shall love." After all, what do we do in our culture when we become impatient with something that is inconvenient? We get rid of it. The liberalization of abortion laws is a prime example of this mentality. Or we may trade in this inconvenient thing for a different one. Living in an era of disposables, exchange and replacement have become so automatic in solving our problems that we apply it to marriage without a second thought.

Actually, isn't remarriage often an exchange or replacement of spouses? I believe this is *always* the case when someone divorces for the purpose of marrying another. We change jobs, homes, cars, churches, and anything else that may become inconvenient or interfere with our comfort and independence. It only follows that one out of three couples "solve" their marriage problems by divorce. They also find new problems equal to or worse than the original ones.

If you are considering divorce, let me advise you to take a close look at what you are doing *before* you start any action. Let me repeat: Most couples get into dissolving their marriages before they realize what is happening.

One business executive I was seeing was having difficulty deciding whether or not to divorce his wife. Although his Christian commitment was not clear to me, he definitely was the conscientious, habitual churchgoing type. Since he was a very pragmatic businessman, I suggested he set up a divorce balance sheet, listing on one side the gains of the divorce and on the other side the losses—including financial.

At our next session he told me without hesitation that he had determined to remain married. From that exercise he realized the problems he had now did not compare with those he would take on in a divorce. His pragmatic decision was very unromantic, but it got him off dead center and again pointed up the truth of the exchange of problems that occurs in a divorce. (Incidentally, with a significant amount of effort from each individual, this couple is again finding romance as well.)

I am aware that there are "exceptional cases" where

physical abuse and threats to life are involved in deciding the future of a marriage. In one church the elders actually had to order a divorce through the courts because of the brutality of a husband who battered his wife over the span of several months. In this case they did well. But let's face the facts: We have made the exception the rule. Divorce in the evangelical church has become "O.K." Not much is said against it any longer. Society has tainted us.

While we continue in our legalism in so many areas where Scripture does *not* speak out, we have become utterly licentious in the matter of divorce—where it *does* speak out. I realize that saving a failing marriage relationship can be a trying, testing experience. But in the end it is worth it. It is time to turn things around and regain righteousness once again. I have written this book to help you truly find the meaning of that permanent union God planned for you in marriage.

For the Christian, divorce is not an option. You promised God and each other that you would stay married for life. Come with me as I show you how it can be done.

Summary

Often couples are so bent on getting out from under the frustrations and pressures of a problem marriage that they do not stop to consider the greater problems of learning to live as a single person again.

Christians need to learn *not* to view divorce as a solution to a rocky marriage and to concentrate instead on how to heal their marriage relationship.

3

Remember? You Promised

June 24, 1960, is like yesterday in my memory. It was a hot summer evening. The ushers were trying to adjust the church doors to allow more air circulation throughout the sanctuary without causing the candles at the front to melt too quickly in the breeze.

Earlier in the day I had helped my father install lightning rods on the top of a barn roof. He owned a rural hardware business and desperately needed my help with that job. Besides, I needed some distracting activity to fill my hours until evening. (I did use the time to practice my wedding vows, for we had decided to memorize them for our ceremony. By the time I had worked halfway across the barn roof, I had my vows down cold.)

The day passed quickly. Now I found myself waiting in a little side room at the front of the church with my brother Glenn, our best man. A door to the outside was propped open, exposing the remnants of a lazy sun which was soon to set behind a large grove of oak trees. I had successfully *acted* calm and somewhat relaxed all day, especially around my brother. But now my heart skipped a beat and I swallowed hard as the organ began sending forth the strains of Bach's "Jesu, Joy of Man's Desiring." I knew my time had finally come.

Just as Glenn started into the sanctuary he pointed to the open door and said with a mischievous grin, "There is your last chance if you want to take it." With that he disappeared into the church. He had a knack of coming up with choice statements at the most opportune (or inopportune) moments.

Alone and waiting to enter, I looked again through the open door to the outside. The sun had now totally disappeared behind the trees. At that moment I realized how alone I felt. Yet, I thought, in a few moments I will be with Judy and I will no longer be alone.

In my heart I said, "Lord, I am ready to make my promise," and with that I passed through the door into the sanctuary, finding myself in front of what seemed like a million people. All I could see were faces and eyes, legions of them, all looking at me.

Even with Glenn beside me I felt alone and very much on display. My eyes moved about the sanctuary, not knowing where to look. One by one the attendants entered.

Then Judy started down the aisle. With our eyes fixed upon each other I became completely unaware of everything else. She had never looked more beautiful. In her white flowing dress, her face delicately hiding behind the bridal veil, she moved gracefully toward me. Right then I wanted to shout and leap for joy. I thought, "Lord, thank You for this beautiful bride You are giving me to be my wife."

The intensity heightened as I reached out and we touched. Judy gently took my arm and together we climbed the stairs of the platform to face the minister. The majestic organ was now silent, and in the hush of the moment the minister said, "Let us pray."

I could easily continue recalling for you detail after

detail of that special evening in our lives. But now I want you to shift your thoughts and images from our wedding to your own. Recall in vivid detail the golden moments of your hour. Let your mind float freely, allowing yourself to remember the events of your wedding that have been tucked away in your memory for years. If you can effectively lose yourself in the history of that day, you will find that you not only recall the facts, but you can also re-experience the feelings.

Try to remember in as much detail as possible your total experiences of that day when *you promised,* before God and witnesses, to love, honor, and cherish your partner in holy wedlock.

The recall potential God has given us is great. The human brain is like a complex computer that has permanently recorded not only facts but also feelings. Therefore it is possible not only to *remember,* but also to *relive* the spontaneous, involuntary feelings of events from our past.

Dr. Wilder Penfield, a neurosurgeon who has done significant research in this area, reports, "Perhaps the most significant discovery was that not only past events are recorded in detail but also the feelings that were associated with those events. An event and the feeling which was produced by the event are inextricably locked together in the brain so that one cannot be evoked without the other."[1]

Apply this principle to yourself and seek out both the facts and feelings of your past. Try to recall those early experiences with your spouse as you grew to know and love each other. If you can really get into it, you will once again find some of the old feelings that accompanied those events that are now history. Returning to the setting where it happened is sure to help. It always happens to us when we visit the church where we met.

Find that compartment in your mind and in this way relive once again *your* wedding day. Can you rediscover the setting and the feelings you had for each other? Do you remember the promises you made? How did you feel as you held your partner's hand and said your vows?

Let me help you recall the promises you made and the meaning behind them.

Dearly beloved, we are gathered together here in the sight of God, and in the presence of these witnesses, to join together this man and this woman in holy matrimony.[2]

If you have not had the experience of serving in public office, in the military, or as a witness in court, your wedding will most likely be the only time in your life when you solemnly and *officially* gave a personal promise. At the onset you were reminded that this moment is not only a human, social, legal event, but also a sacred one: "In the sight of God." God was present and was very much a part of your very special moment. His presence continues throughout your marriage.

As the ceremony continued, you were asked to:

. . . love, comfort, honor and keep him/her, in sickness and in health; and, forsaking all others, keep thee only unto him/her, so long as you both shall live?[3]

This makes the answer to the question of the third-party affair distinctly clear. You clearly stated there would be no one else for the rest of your life. At the time, when your relationship was new and fresh, forsaking others was an easy task. But *you promised* to continue forsaking others and to love one another day after day, month after month, year after year, "so long as you both shall live."

No one is above temptation, but the Bible gives very clear direction on what to do when tempted. The apostle Paul tells young Timothy, "Run from anything that gives you the evil thoughts that young men often have, but stay close to anything that makes you want to do right."[4] We are told not to *casually avoid,* but to *boldly run* from evil. This lesson is demonstrated in the Bible when Potiphar's wife attempted to seduce young handsome Joseph. Let's read the account.

Then one day as he was in the house going about his work—as it happened, no one else was around at the time—she came and grabbed him by the sleeve demanding, "Sleep with me." He tore himself away, but as he did, his jacket slipped off and she was left holding it as he fled from the house.[5]

In order to remain faithful to one, there are times when you must literally run from the temptation of others.

Please note one other subtle point in these two examples. If Timothy and Joseph were obedient by running or fleeing the temptation, then surely they must have *felt* the temptation. The lesson is this: *The problem is not the feelings, but rather our behavior in response to those feelings.* Behavior and feelings are often confused as being the same, when actually they are very different.

Feelings are involuntary emotional responses to a situation. They are neither good nor bad, but they are real. Behavior is an action response to a feeling. The Bible instructs us about how to respond to a given feeling. In this situation we are told to flee, run, or get away from the temptation as quickly as possible.

Somehow we who call ourselves evangelical Christians have all but forgotten perseverance to commitments we have made. Vows and covenants are no longer chic in our modern theology. Only God makes promises—not us. This same mentality has influenced the way many Christians do business. Time and again I have heard people say, "I'd rather do business with a non-Christian any day—unbelievers are more dependable."

You may try to rationalize your reasons for seeking "greener pastures." I have heard many in my office, and some are very convincing. But whatever your reasons, there is one fact you cannot rationalize away. *You gave your word. You promised* to "forsake all others for as long as you both shall live." God will hold you to it.

Then you said:

I,_____, take thee _____ to be my wedded husband/wife, to have and to hold from this day forward, for better, for worse, for richer, for poorer, in sickness and in health, to love and to cherish, till death us do part.[6]

Judy always smiles as she recalls this portion of the vows. In spite of all my rehearsing earlier in the day on the barn roof, I still managed to leave out "in sickness" as I repeated the words from memory.

After I had finished, she quietly whispered, "You forgot to say 'in sickness.'"

Without a ruffle I quietly replied, "That too!"

We both jokingly comment now that the omission must have had a positive affect on her health. At age sixteen she had been flat on her back for six months with a severe case of rheumatic fever. At that time the doctor told her she would always have to take things easy and learn to watch the rest of the world go by. Since we have been married, however, she has given birth to our three children and runs a very busy household, including (voluntarily!) cutting the grass in the summer and clearing the driveway of snow in the winter.

For Better, for Worse. Here we have two unlimited extremes. Believe it or not, "for better" should not be passed over lightly. There are special temptations when things are "better." Laziness, complacency, and boredom can enter, bringing about decay in the relationship. These factors are often the result of success and the abundance of comfort without much effort on your part. I am sure you can think of a couple who shocked you by getting a divorce. The typical comment is, "They seemed so happy and had everything going for them." Remember, there are subtle hazards in the "for better" part of your marriage.

What are the limits of "for worse"? This is the question I am often asked by persons in marital difficulty. According to the vows you made, the "for worse" is not qualified or limited in any way. "That's not fair. We did not know what we were getting into at the time," some complain. Nevertheless, if you decide to terminate your marriage because the relationship is "for worse," you must abandon your vows and break your promise.

One Christian man who has given his life to propagating the gospel, and who seriously flirted with leaving his wife and family, gives very pointed advice to those who excuse themselves with past misjudgments: "Stop blaming your past for your present condition; accept responsibility for your own behavior. Most things that we don't like about ourselves *can* be changed with God's help."

That's no platitude! He and his wife, giving the glory to Jesus Christ, did just that. In the face of difficulties, which had been building up virtually since their marriage began, they turned from their hardness to one another and are making their "for worses" better!

For Richer, for Poorer. Money is a subject everyone relates to. Most people do not have "enough." But when the question comes up, "How much do we need?" the universal reply seems to be, "Just a little bit more." Most of us can identify with this condition. But wealth can also bring problems. The Scriptures teach that the love of money is the root of all evil.

A young wife with whom I have been counseling for quite some time came into my office the other day with a new problem. She said, "I'm worried because my husband feels he has to earn seven-and-a-half million dollars before he can let up."

Her concern is not without grounds. He will probably do it! He is a very successful businessman who already has earned nearly his first million. She explained that his figures show he must have over seven million dollars before he can be financially independent. For this woman, "for richer" is squeezing her out of his life.

Having had the opportunity to counsel with several very wealthy couples, I have learned about other hazards that accompany the "for richer" category. These couples often find that their wealth takes more and more control of them instead of them controlling their wealth. Their world revolves around the making and spending of money. I often recall in these situations the words of James:

Look here, you people who say, "Today or tomorrow we are going to such and such a town, stay there a year, and open up a profitable business." How do you know what is going to happen tomorrow? For the length of your lives is as uncertain as the morning fog—now you see it; soon it is gone.[7]

Because of their money, the rich seem to need less of each other. The personal attention and services given and received by the spouses in most wealthy marriages are often purchased. The cook prepares the meals, the gardener does the yard, the secretary buys the gifts, and the party is provided by the country club. In a later chapter you will learn how relationships are built on meeting one another's needs. When the satisfaction of needs is *purchased,* the relationship is formed with the money rather than with the spouse.

"For poorer" is the category most of us identify with. Our response depends largely upon *when* in the marriage we are poor. In the early stages it is acceptable. You may still be in school, new in your job, starting your own business, or making other preparations for your career. *You have not yet had a chance to fail.*

In our society of free enterprise, the possession of material goods implies having money. Money indicates earning power, which symbolizes success. Therefore, the more years you add to your marriage the more difficult it will become to remain contented in the "for poorer" group. But in your vows, the "for poorer" was not qualified—it may mean "for poorer" until death us do part!

In Sickness and in Health. "She has had seven major surgeries and spent the majority of the last ten years in and out of hospitals. Many of these illnesses were unrelated and, as she would recover from one, another would develop. Holidays were frequently celebrated in a hospital room and their growing son's achievements were reported secondhand by her husband. At the end of all this, she is still not well. Most of her illness is chronic, and she was told by doctors that she will have to learn to live with the pain and discomfort. Nothing more can be done." A disheartening report to be sure.

But these two Christians are living out their vows "to

37

love and to cherish in sickness . . . till death us do part."
Today they are more in love than ever before. Interested
friends have asked them if they ever get discouraged in the
midst of their trials.

"More than you will ever know," they respond. "But
we have learned to express our anger and other negative
feelings toward the illness and not toward the person who
is ill."

How easy it is for a chronically ill person to feel guilty
over his illness, the trouble he causes other people, and his
lack of response to treatment. Any negative feelings expressed by the healthy spouse regarding the illness are
often taken personally, thus feeding the guilt.

Remember that your body is the temple of the Holy
Spirit. Whether your body is sick or healthy, the Holy
Spirit lives within you.

Here is what Scripture tells us:

Haven't you yet learned that your body is the home of the
Holy Spirit God gave you, and that he lives within you? Your
own body does not belong to you. For God has bought you with
a great price. So use every part of your body to give glory back
to God, because he owns it.[8]

God the Holy Spirit dwells within the body of the
Christian. He is present regardless of your physical
health. God has promised this unconditionally. In like
manner you made the same promise in your wedding
vows: "to love and to cherish in *sickness* and in health till
death us do part."

One day I asked this same couple why they are so close
and so much in love. As they were pondering their response, I more specifically asked the husband why he had
never divorced his wife. His response was simple but very

profound: "Well, after all we *are* married and she *is* my wife." They made a promise they intended to keep!

It was several days later when I saw them the next time, and the wife said she had more of an answer for me. After thinking about my question almost constantly since I had last seen them, she had finally concluded that their marriage is not founded on romantic love, but rather on a carefully developed intimacy. "Romantic love is there," she said, "but it comes and goes with the moods of the situation. It is the intimacy of deeply knowing each other and unconditionally accepting each other that really forms the basis of our relationship."

Then *I* had to think about *her* comment for several days. Previously, I had thought it must be the patience and understanding they tried to maintain toward each other through these trying years that kept them going. But that was not it at all. Rather it was the freedom to show the pain, depression, extreme anger, frustration, and giving up on everything only to hope again. It was this *freedom* of honest expression to all the *feelings* and *thoughts*— especially the negative, unpleasant ones—in which the seeds of intimacy were planted and grew into a strong marriage relationship. Although her body is sick and weak, their relationship is strong and healthy, filled with beauty and life.

Whether or not you experience illness or whether your problems are job failure or obesity, with this same process you can develop an intimacy that provides the strong foundation for your marriage.

Is it becoming more clear why your vows are so important? Intimacy, the foundation of a relationship, cannot develop unless you are truly free to be yourself. You cannot be yourself totally unless you know your partner unconditionally accepts you and will always be there.

So Long as You Both Shall Live. Marriage is a *lifetime* proposition. Anything less than that is not God's way. In Genesis we are told:

This explains why a man leaves his father and mother and is joined to his wife in such a way that the two become one person.[9]

The man and woman do not become "as one" or "similar to being one," but indeed *are* one flesh. This is a new entity, a shared human nature, a creation ordained by God and compared to the love relationship of all love relationships, Christ and the church. To experience what the intimacy of marriage really is, your promise must be unconditional—which means it is for a lifetime.

Many young couples today are revising their vows. One of the more common revisions is, as we have noted, to replace the word *live* with *love*. The vows then read, "so long as we both shall love." That simple change of one small word completely alters what you promise. It makes a conditional promise out of one that must be unconditional. What you are saying is that your promise holds true only as long as you are aware of a love for your partner.

Anyone who has been married a few years knows that the awareness of the presence of romantic love waxes and wanes in the dynamic changes that go on constantly in that intimate relationship. In the heat of an argument, the feelings of romantic love often become confused and distorted. *Conditional vows of this type plant a seed of insecurity right from the beginning.*

Lack of commitment and the *deterioration of a relationship* go hand in hand. While sitting in group therapy one night, someone noticed that only one person in the entire group was wearing a wedding ring. Being the therapist in the group, I wished I had been perceptive enough to make that observation. However, I felt it was significant that a group member who was not wearing a ring pointed it out to the rest of us.

The group picked up on it and through discussion learned that each person had a definite reason for removing the ring. Every one of them reflected on a time when they began to withdraw trust and commitment from the other. (Incidentally, the one person wearing his ring was a husband who had expressed a certainty of his love for his wife and was trying, without doubt, to save his marriage. He was committed to her.) The lesson here is that the absence of commitment, sometimes symbolized by the absence of wedding rings, is a common denominator for most couples having marital problems.

Try to recall those moments *after* your vows were said. You were probably wearing a shiny new wedding ring. Your spouse probably had to have your help in putting it on your finger during the ceremony. Or if you were like me, you left it stuck halfway on your finger until the pastor prayed. Then when no one was looking, you slipped it on the rest of the way.

After the benediction, the church bells rang and you turned around arm in arm to face the congregation and the world. For the first time you officially heard your names as Mr. and Mrs. when the pastor publicly introduced you. It seemed like the longest moment in history from that time until the organist started the recessional.

Can you remember—or better yet—*relive* in your heart the feelings you shared as you hurried up the aisle as husband and wife? I trust that, as with us, your joy was complete; for your commitment was fresh and full of meaning. The knot had been tied not only at the church but also in heaven.

Summary

I am convinced that a primary reason Christian marriages are breaking up is that we have become hardened toward the validity of a *promise* made before God and man. Whether we like it or not, such a promise as that made in marriage is eternally binding, and we will be held to it before the judgment seat of Christ.

At this point in history—when even many Christians are living by convenience—may God give us obedient, tender hearts to forsake our sins of doing what is right in our own eyes, and return again with obedience to the promises we have made, whatever the cost.

4

God Designed You to Be Married

A single glance into the waiting room was sufficient to identify the person I would be seeing for the first time in counseling that morning. His newness to this situation was evident as he tried to blend in with the regulars who had been coming weeks, months, and even years.

To most people this large-statured, well-dressed businessman appeared impeccable in every respect, even down to his well-trimmed, slightly graying mustache. But to those of us who are experienced in inviting people from the waiting room into our offices, he gave himself away. He held an outdated magazine from the nearby table, flipping the pages as though he were intensely interested. His eyes, however, seemed to look at everything in the room except the pages before him. They moved quickly from face to face so as not to appear as though he were staring at the others. Yet silently he seemed to be asking himself, "I wonder why they are here?"

Almost as a conditioned response, he vaulted to his feet when he heard me call his name and charged toward me with his hand extended. He was showing me a phony confidence I am certain he had practiced and groomed for years as a sales executive. What he did not realize was that in his other hand he was still clutching the magazine that had been his security during the wait.

Taking the chair closest to the door in my office, he sat down and with a slight twinge of embarrassment laid the magazine on the floor beside him. Sitting silently, I allowed him to settle into the quiet privacy of the office. He seemed relieved to be here, but he was anxious about where all this therapy might lead. In only a matter of moments his well-developed defenses began to evaporate. The confident, aggressive businessman who gave every outward sign of success was gradually transformed into a frightened, insecure person showing traces of panic across his face.

I let my eyes do the talking as I patiently waited for his first words. In a barely audible whisper he said, "I don't know who I really am." His eyes moved slowly from the floor in front of him to the window and a small lake behind the clinic. In a slightly stronger voice, but still preoccupied in his thoughts, he continued, "I don't even know what I am like." Then, realizing that I was in the room with him, his eyes searched mine as he said, "I feel I'm all alone."

As we talked, I could see that this person had all the outward appearances of everything a man could want. He was married and had three healthy children and a successful, growing business. Recently he and his family had moved into a new house and had it furnished by a professional decorator. He had all the evidences of success. Yet he was searching.

"I know what I need," he finally said near the close of our session.

"What?" I asked, hoping he was sensing what had become apparent to me.

"I need a close personal relationship," he replied.

It seemed as if he should have had several, but in the demands of his business lifestyle he had always set them aside. Now it was catching up with him. In the sessions that followed I worked with him as he successfully developed his personal relationships, of which his marriage was the first.

What this man discovered to be his basic need is not unique to him. We all need at least one close personal relationship, and much of our activity and behavior is centered on finding and maintaining that relationship. For most of us this relationship is ideally found in our marriage, but for some it is found elsewhere.

For some of you it may be God's will that you remain single. Others of you have become single through the death of your spouse. But whether or not you are married, everyone needs to have at least one close personal relationship. If you do not, you will have a sense of loneliness.

Loneliness, the absence of relationships, can hurt you physically as well as emotionally. Relationships are essential to your physical health. Dr. James J. Lynch, a specialist in psychosomatic medicine, tells us that the absence of relationships brings emotional and then physical deterioration. Human touch and caring has a profound effect on a person's recovery from illness. He further points out that doctors and others must make people aware that family life is as important to health as is diet and exercise. Without question, Dr. Lynch reports, there is a biological basis for our need to form human relationships, and if we fail to fulfill that need our health is in peril.[1] Let's face it: we need relationships to survive.

This is why divorced people tell of being so incredibly lonely. They have once known the intimacy of a warm, close relationship and now it exists no longer. The emptiness and hollowness that comes after a marriage is dissolved can be almost devastating, and the last state of the divorce is often far worse than the first.

One newly divorced man, a most active and productive Christian, wrote, "I yearn to come home to a house that is a home—full of life and love and laughter. Instead, my house is empty, my bed is cold, my children no longer come home to me. I find it extremely difficult to admit that my family will never be back together again, that my children will never live with me, and that I will possibly have to live alone the rest of my life."

As we examine why Christian marriages are failing, we need to know why people choose to get married in the first place. What motivates someone to marry? What motivates people to leave a life of singleness and independence to enter a relationship for a lifetime? What leads people to accept the controls, limits, and expectations that are placed on them by another person, another family, and by society as a whole?

I believe the answer lies in the importance of relationships in our lives. At the risk of becoming too theoretical, I would like to spend the remainder of this chapter showing you exactly how much your relationships mean to you. Please stay with me, for the principles I am about to discuss will be the foundation for the rest of the book.

Relationships are essential to your well-being. Through them you find answers to the questions "Who am I?" and "What am I like?" The relationships you have and your ability to form the ones you need is the key to finding your self-identity and your self-esteem. You cannot know who you are or how you feel about yourself without having an understanding of how other people see you.

You determine what you are like by how others perceive you. The presence or the addition of new relationships creates happiness and usually a good self-concept. On the other hand, their absence or loss brings about dejection and a loss of self-worth.

This truth was vividly illustrated to me the other day by my daughter, who is just six years old. (Children are great teachers. Their feelings are still right on the surface. They have not yet had the opportunity to develop a sophisticated defensive system to cover their true emotions.)

As it happened this particular afternoon, Leah came into the house in tears. She was crying so hard that I was certain she had been seriously hurt. I met Judy at the kitchen door and as we both dashed to her rescue we said simultaneously, "Leah, what happened?"

Relieved at first at the absence of any scrapes or blood, we listened intently as she blurted out between sobs, "I have no friends. No one will play with me."

The tears streaming down her face and her sobs made us realize her hurt was more severe than two skinned knees *and* a bump on the head. Her hurt feelings were right there where everyone could see them and respond. As I held her, reassuring her that I would be her friend, I wondered about all the big kids we call "adults" all over the world today who are crying like Leah because they have no friends. Of course, their sobs are carefully hidden behind cosmetic smiles, safely out of the reach of anyone who might respond.

The ending to this story can be told quickly. Two hours later, Leah went through the house laughing and singing. Yes, two friends were following her.

Not only are relationships important in discovering who you are, they also play a vital role in meeting your basic needs. What are these basic needs? Dr. William Glasser, a psychiatrist and founder of reality therapy, defines them as (1) to love and be loved and (2) to feel worthwhile to yourself and others.[2]

According to Dr. Glasser, all our behavior revolves around these two basic emotional needs. One logical conclusion can be drawn from this principle: Relationships are required to meet these needs. Only then will you experience loving, being loved, and knowing that you are indeed worthwhile.

Your relationships are formed and sustained by what I call a "mutual need-meeting activity." Think of a relationship that you have and examine how it formed and what keeps it going. In the beginning you met some of this person's needs, and in turn he met some of yours. The more needs that are successfully met, the stronger the relationship becomes. In contrast, the fewer the needs that are met in both directions, the weaker the relationship becomes. If you become skillful in responding to the needs of others, I guarantee that you will have relationships.

Let me emphasize here that by need-meeting I do not mean a selfish, self-centered stance where you are out for what you can get. Rather, it starts as an expression of giving. After all, the Bible teaches us that giving produces greater happiness than receiving.[3] But as you begin giving to someone, it is natural for them to give in return. When this happens you have a relationship. When it doesn't, a relationship will not form. If there was one, it will not continue, but will weaken and fall apart. The same is true in your marriage.

Here is an example of how this worked for us with our neighbors. One family in our neighborhood seemed to have almost every material possession a family could ever want. Our friendship was cordial, but not particularly close. Then one fall day as we were putting away our summer yard equipment, I noticed my neighbor had a need

I could meet. He had a paddle boat that needed to be stored for the winter, and I had the storage space.

By storing his boat for him a chain of exchanges was started whereby we both have benefited from the other's favors. From this a relationship has been strengthened. Obviously, the relationship is really built on the emotional needs that are met in the process of our doing favors for each other.

You cannot fully understand your human relationships until you have a relationship with God, your Creator. God wants and invites us to have a relationship with Him. This must come first.

The Old Testament prophet recorded about God's Word: "I don't want your sacrifices—I want your love; I don't want your offerings—I want you to know Me."[4] The message could not have been clearer. At a time in Israel's history when sacrifices and offerings had degenerated into mere form, God rejected them and called His people back to a relationship with Him. His priority is clear. God wants our love. He wants us to know Him. Furthermore, He wants us to love one another as He has loved us.[5]

Most relationships do not last for a lifetime. New ones are formed and others end. Those relationships that do last will go through many stages of change. Both are normal situations of life. However, when a relationship changes it has an emotional effect upon you. Usually your strongest feelings are directly connected to the beginning or ending of a relationship. You change jobs. You move to a new neighborhood. Parents die. Children grow up. Relationships continue to change.

In the midst of all this you need a constant, stable relationship to carry you through a lifetime of changes, one that remains constant when everything else seems to be in a state of flux.

This is where the marriage relationship comes in. A responsive, constant marriage relationship will provide for you confidence, stability, and security. When everything else lets you down, your marriage assures you that you are loved and worthwhile to at least one person—your marriage partner. If you are not married and God wills for you to remain single, this relationship will be provided in some other form. On the other hand, if you are married and your marriage is failing, you can see how the very foundation of your stability is being shaken.

The stability that a marriage relationship can provide is unique. Marriage *is* the relationship of relationships. In the United States today, about 95 percent of all men and women marry.[6] In spite of the problems the institution of marriage is facing in our society, it is fascinating to see that people still prefer a lifestyle of marriage as opposed to singleness.

What is even more astonishing is that most people who experience marriage failure and divorce choose to try again. Of all the women under forty who divorce, 90 percent eventually remarry. Divorced men are more likely to remarry than are divorced women, thereby putting them in an even higher percentage.[7] My point here is not to deal with the question of remarriage, but to show that most people have a strong need for the constant committed relationship of marriage even though they may have previously failed at it.

God intends almost everyone to be married, including Carol, who has a happy ending to a story that was filled with problems. I have known her now for nearly four years. She came to me the first time after seeing her family doctor because she had been experiencing some strange physical symptoms. She had been bothered by double vision and numbness in her feet.

After undergoing a variety of neurological tests, this very attractive, energetic young nurse was told that she had multiple sclerosis, a chronic disease of the nervous system often resulting in increased physical disability. Many people with this malady end up in a wheelchair with varying degrees of paralysis. For others, the symptoms remain minimal for years. Since this was Carol's situation, she could continue working as a nursing instructor.

To my surprise, when I talked with Carol in that initial session she said she was accepting the illness just fine. It was her marriage that she could not figure out. Her husband had withdrawn and was becoming more distant and noncommunicative. In one brief session with him alone, he told me he wanted a divorce and made it clear he was not interested in marriage counseling. His reasons for wanting to end the marriage were vague, puzzling both Carol and me. Because of the timing of his decision, however, I was led to believe he was running scared and afraid of spending a lifetime with an invalid wife.

He did leave her. My contacts with Carol continued over the years, helping her cope with the single life she had never wanted nor asked for.

Not long ago I received one of those telephone calls that leaves anyone in my business in total suspense. The call was from Carol. With a puzzled excitement she said, "Jerry, you will never guess what is happening to me!" The long silence that followed indicated one of those rare moments in my life when I have nothing to say as my mind searches frantically for the appropriate reply. Unable to wait for my response, she blurted out, "I'm getting married!" Trying to remain professional, yet elated with the news, I agreed to meet with them before they tied the knot.

The session was a beautiful experience. Rarely do I find myself meeting with couples who are happy and very much in love. Carol's future husband, who had never been married, was a doctor trained in the specialty of physical medicine, which will be extremely helpful to Carol. Their love for one another was obvious to anyone. As they were leaving my office, Carol turned to me with a glow of happiness on her face that I had never seen before and said, "Let's face it, Jerry. I was just meant to be married!"

I thought, "Yes, Carol, you and almost everyone else."

Summary

Christian marriages are breaking up because couples do not understand the importance of relationships and the need to actively maintain their marriage relationship through meeting one another's needs. God made them to be joined in marriage specifically with their mate. They lose sight of the fact that they will be far more fulfilled in a marriage where problems are dealt with together than back in a single state with a whole new set of problems to face alone.

Agree with God that it is not His will for you to be alone. For most of you it is His will that you find completion in marriage. For singles and widows, He will provide that special relationship (or relationships) unqiue for your situation.

5

Too Good to Be Real

Many Christian husbands and wives are really strangers to each other. As we saw in the last chapter, they have never allowed their marriage to become the truly intimate relationship it was intended to be. Having experienced rejection previously when their negative side was revealed to others, they have chosen in their marriage to disclose only a part of themselves—the good part. It is easy to show patience, kindness, self-confidence, and the other traits that have successfully passed the acceptance test of others. Fears, anger, insecurities, and other traits that are considered negative remain safely concealed behind defensive walls, out of the reach of their partners.

I'll never forget the shock I encountered personally when a couple, who were my close Christian friends, announced they were getting a divorce. They were in their mid-thirties, and for years had hosted an exciting Bible study in their home. In fact the group had become so large, and so many people had made professions of faith in Jesus Christ, that they had had a huge room built on the back of the house just to hold everyone.

This couple was, as they say in the South, part of the "blue blood" of the city. Both were from prominent families. She had been a beauty queen; he was repeatedly elected to state government posts. In these capacities, they had both borne consistent verbal witness.

When the news of the divorce became public, I had a chance to visit with the wife and ask her, "Why?" She told me how she and her husband had always been at the top of everything they had ever tried to do. He loved her award-winning beauty; she saw him as her ideal public leader and spiritual stalwart. But their relationship never grew. When she probed her mind to produce a one-sentence answer to my question, she said, "I guess we fell in love with each other's image."

Their marriage, the burgeoning study group and, you guessed it, even a number of the new converts all went down the drain.

Showing your good characteristics and concealing your negative ones is a pattern that starts early in life. From infancy you are taught this both in what you are told and in what you see other people do. One of those early messages may have been, "Be careful what you do. What will people think?" As you became skillful at determining what people thought, you learned that they liked your good characteristics and rejected your negative feelings in various ways.

If you are like most of us, this message was repeated over and over throughout childhood until by the time you were grown up no one needed to tell you anymore. You now have a recording of it in your head, and it plays all by itself even when you wish it would not.

This pattern of concealment of negative feelings can become so integrated into a person's behavior that he is unaware he is doing it. Others will notice something is lacking in the relationship, but don't know what it is. You are relating to only a *part* of a person—the good part. And that is *too good to be real.*

Concealing your negative feelings is not always bad. Relationships among single people are never intended to handle that level of openness. I have counseled with many single persons who have revealed too much of themselves too quickly, resulting in hurt and rejection. Your personality defenses that cover many of your needs and feelings are very useful in protecting your self-esteem as a relationship is being formed. One of the exciting aspects of a new relationship is watching it grow as each person progressively divulges more and more of himself or herself.

Marriage, however, is a different story. Since it is intended to be the most intimate of all relationships, it is essential that you know all of your partner—the good and the bad. For many this is a very difficult task. They would rather expose only their good side, knowing that by doing this acceptance is guaranteed. After all, that is what they were taught and it has worked in other relationships for years. Although it will also work in marriage, by sharing only a part of yourself you are seriously limiting the relationship and creating a superficial marriage.

In this superficial relationship you will talk comfortably about the neighbors, your job, world events, almost anything as long as you stay away from discussing each other. "We talk," as some of my couples have come to call it, is more difficult. This subject unquestionably will lead you to that special private material in yourself that has been tucked away for years behind your walls. The conversation does not come easily, but the positive effect on your relationship will make it worth the effort.

One Christian minister, whose once shaky marriage is being restored, advises: "Take time to get to know about your mate's past. Hold nothing back, or if anything is held back, assume personal responsibility that what is being held back is not detrimental to a good understanding of yourself by your mate. Find out what things in the past hurt, felt good, and brought hope. Start immediately to learn how to discuss ideas and feelings in an accepting, noncondemning frame of reference."

He continues, "I would not have allowed my wife's feelings of insecurity to go unchallenged and untreated for as long as I did. Being 'patient' in that way with a mate is not good for them. They need to work toward changes in their lives of those things that are detrimental to the marriage.

"I would have learned better ways to explain why I am the person I am. I would have tried harder to communicate on a feelings level instead of descending into the same old circular arguments on the basis of cold facts! 'You did! I didn't! Yes, you did! No, I didn't,' etc."

More than anyone else, the Christian has the potential to be open, honest, and very real with his feelings. Yet I have found the opposite to be true. Growing up as one committed to Christ and knowing many who love the Lord, I have come to realize that we are conditioned even more than others to keep our negative side concealed. We have an obsessive preoccupation with how we appear to others. If we have a problem or need that may reflect failure or weakness, especially in our faith, our first concern is not to resolve the problem; rather, it is to make sure that no one finds out.

Why is the Christian, more than other people, likely to appear *too good to be real?* Because in reality he is! Look at what God's Word tells us about perfection. "For by that one offering he made forever perfect in the sight of God all those whom he is making holy."[1]

Theologians tell us this verse points out that in the eyes of God we are indeed perfect. However, let us remember that we are perfected by a single offering—the shed blood of Jesus Christ, the Son of God. God sees us as perfect through His Son. Therefore, our perfection is based on *our relationship with the Lord,* not on *what we do.* Our Christian behavior is not the source of our perfection; it is the result of it.

Both our Christian behavior and our loving relationship with God are important, but we tend to get the order reversed. After we have become totally aware of God's love for us, an open, honest relationship of faith and trust must come first. The behavior follows as a natural response to that relationship.

The same is true in your marriage. The relationship of love and trust must be established first. Then loving behavior follows as a natural response to that firmly established intimate relationship. This will happen only as you get to know more and more about each other. Your partner is allowed the opportunity to accept and understand some intimate parts of yourself that you were sure he or she would reject.

How well I remember a couple who were encountering this situation. The silence was heavy between each word that was eventually spoken by a very guilty wife. Slowly she told her story. Her husband had reassured her of his love, but as yet she had not tested it. The test was happening now as she unfolded a story about herself that she was certain would lead to his rejection of her.

But it didn't. He listened with caring. After she finished, she broke into tears and threw herself into his arms. There had been no physical expressions of affection between them for months, but now the love expressed verbally had been tested. An intimate relationship was firmly established and loving behavior naturally followed.

As a way of staying away from their needs and feelings during those first sessions, most couples I see tend to focus on the other's behavior, or on "who does what." By the time they come to see me, they are often getting tired of doing all those good things that are unappreciated by their partner. Finally becoming fed up, they decide it is time to expect something in return. They come to me, expecting a referee or negotiator with all the wisdom to offer supreme fairness.

At first they continue to spar with each other, pointing out all the good they are giving to the relationship and the little they are receiving in return. What they are doing is avoiding their *real* needs and feelings about themselves and each other.

Often these couples will become irritated with me since, in spite of all my professional wisdom, I do not come up with the decree as to who should carry out the garbage. However, as the sessions progress the focus moves from these surface issues to removing the walls and showing the feelings that they were sure would never be understood. Often to the couple's surprise, as these emotions are shared and not rejected, the garbage somehow seems to get carried out—usually by the one who walks through the kitchen and notices that the container is full!

A marriage relationship is not built on negotiated behavior, but rather on an intimacy that develops from communicating emotional needs and feelings, both the good and the negative ones.

How does it affect you when you are around someone you care about and they will not let you get close to them? You probably find that you become impatient and then downright angry. You see, hostility and defensiveness go hand in hand. One person's defensiveness brings out hostility in another person.

You can always count on the people in a therapy group to show honest reactions to a person's behavior. Predictably, anger is kindled in the members when one of them becomes defensive and shuts out the rest of the group.

As a matter of fact, anger is an emotion I must often deal with in myself as I counsel with a defensive person. I have come to the conclusion that a person's defensiveness is essentially a rejection of *you*. The defensive person is doing to you exactly what they are afraid you will do to them. By their defensiveness they are telling you that they do not trust you and your response to what they might reveal. Actually, you are being shut out.

Can you see what this does in a marriage? If the husband, for example, is defensive about some feelings, his wife will begin to get angry and feel shut out. Threatened by his wife's anger, his natural response is to close off even further, which in turn causes his wife to become even more angry. The process is a vicious downward spiral that often ends in a violent argument, or more destructive yet—total withdrawal.

This cause-and-effect process of defensiveness and anger is one of the most common problems in Christian marriages. Its basis is in the initial decision of one of the partners not to be open with some needs or feelings that are necessary for the relationship to grow. And I believe *this all goes back to Christians viewing perfection as never sinning, instead of seeing perfection as the ability to receive forgiveness in the pursuit of righteousness.*

Early one Monday morning I received a telephone call from a pastor in our community. I knew this man quite well and routinely saw referrals from him. This time he said it was a somewhat different situation.

The couple he was calling about were strangers to him. They had chosen not to go to their own pastor, fearing his knowledge of their problems. They had carefully selected someone from the other side of the city. Furthermore, they wanted to meet with a Christian counselor who did not know their pastor or the people from their church.

Because I met these qualifications, he asked if I would be willing to counsel them. Even though I had not yet met them, I was already sensing in myself some resentment toward their defensiveness. However, as a favor to my pastor friend and due to my basic commitment to see any couple for at least one session, I somewhat reluctantly accepted the referral and scheduled their first appointment.

When they arrived, it was even worse than I had anticipated. As I picked up the new file containing some general information that we ask from all new referrals, my receptionist said, "Good luck. I'm glad it's you and not I who's meeting with them!"

It was a very significant comment, for she is an extremely patient person whose tolerance almost never allows her to make such a caustic statement unless someone has really given her a hard time.

Observing this couple through the glass in the waiting-room door, I saw two tense, hostile people sitting in opposite corners of the room, like fighters in a ring awaiting the bell to begin round one. I would not have known they were together if they had not been the only two persons in the waiting room at that time.

I took a deep breath, cleared my throat, and opened the door to call their names. From the far corner of the room, the husband darted toward me as if he were racing his wife, although he never once glanced at her. As he approached, he asked curtly, "Which office?"

Almost as a natural reflex I replied, "First one on the left." Without missing a step, he went by me as if he worked there and disappeared into my office.

Meanwhile, I was still standing there holding open the

door for his wife, who deliberately seemed to be taking her time gathering up her purse, sweater, two books, and a tablet with what appeared to be a list of grievances regarding her husband. She said nothing as she stood rigidly and started toward me. Her face was strained, her lips drawn so tightly together that her mouth appeared permanently sealed shut. (I later learned this was not true!)

As she passed me at the door her stone face shifted to a forced smile—one of those courtesy gestures—that seemed to be a major effort. The smile was so brief that I am certain I would have missed it if I had blinked! I took one last glance at my receptionist, whose reassuring look told me she would remain no matter what happened during the next hour.

As I closed the door and sat down, I saw two tightly-coiled springs ready to be released. They watched me as if they expected me to fire the starting gun to open their verbal contest. What I did not realize was that the gun went off when I said, "Who would like to tell me why you are here?"

The husband won the start by saying he would go first, and without wasting a breath he began his list of complaints about what his wife did not do for the marriage, at the same time emphasizing how hard he was trying. He got no further than the second point when his wife began interrupting with denials and clarifications on each of his accusations. While reclarifying her clarifications, confusion hit and they were into one of their inevitable, nonproductive fights.

Between the shouts and the tears there was a lull. This was my moment. Profoundly I declared that it was certainly clear to me that they needed to be here, to which they both agreed. (If you can get people like this to agree on anything, I consider it progress. Besides, that *safe* statement kept me in a neutral position. You see, when you are around hostile, defensive people there is a natural tendency to become cautious and a little defensive yourself.)

After listening for over half of the session to their shouts, tears, and exchanges of accusations, each one protecting himself from the other, I asked if they had any idea how the other one was feeling.

Between her tears and sobs the wife replied, "He doesn't have any feelings."

"What do you know about feelings?" he shot back. "All you are interested in is what I do or don't do to please you."

Then I asked, "Are you trying to tell us that you do have some feelings you aren't talking about?"

After a brief hesitation, he replied, "Yes."

There was something different in that reply. He had said that one little three-letter word in a tone of voice I had not heard from him before. It came out quietly and honestly.

Now the office was so quiet we could hear each other breathing. Another unusual thing was happening: he had his wife's undivided attention, something he had been trying for unsuccessfully since the session began. Gently I asked him why he had not talked about them before.

After more silence, two more words slipped from his lips, "I'm afraid."

Like an echo came a reply from the other voice in the room, "Me, too."

Two individuals who previously had conducted simultaneous filibusters to protect themselves from the verbal attack of the other now sat speechless. They silently looked at each other as frightened strangers in a new territory. I knew, and so did they, that they were being open and honest with their feelings for the first time in who knows how long. They knew now what it was to be real. Intimacy had been established, and they were on their way.

This experience was also profound for me, for I became aware of how frightening it really is for some people to be open. I also noted how dramatically *my* feelings changed toward this couple as they dropped their defensiveness and revealed some of their real feelings.

This couple continue to see me in weekly sessions. In the beginning I was certain they were a "one-session couple," but what started in the first appointment was a process of growing trust in one another as well as in others. Through this growth, they are experiencing a joy in their marriage that is totally new for them. They still have a long way to go, but believe it or not I enjoy seeing them each week.

Behind all defensiveness is fear—fear of not being accepted or understood. Knowing this, I try to reach beyond defensiveness to the fear itself. You need to do this in your marriage as well. It can be done if you do not allow your intolerance of the guardedness to overtake your efforts to understand. To attack the defense is counterproductive; it heightens and reinforces those protective walls. By showing understanding, the walls are no longer needed.

The *fear of rejection* or not being accepted is no doubt the most powerful of all fears to our psychological state. We become acquainted with this fear early in life, and it becomes increasingly pronounced during our adolescent years.

Think back to that time when you asked that cute young girl out for a date. Remember how you experienced the anxiety and agony over the possibility of her saying *no?* Nothing could have been worse! My wife tells me women go through this same anguish just waiting to be asked. We may laugh about it now, but the feelings were real then and the impact was great.

The other night I happened to watch a television talk show during which one of Hollywood's very masculine actors was being interviewed. This man's fame has come through playing roles of fearlessness in the face of danger. It was interesting to note as he talked on the show that this trait is part of his real life as well. He said that he acquired it because he is very familiar with success, seldom failing at whatever he does. Being previously married and divorced, he was asked if he ever intended to marry again. To my surprise he said, "No, I failed at it once and it scares me."

Rejection is powerful, and the fear of it touches everyone, even the strongest. John Powell sums it up in the question that became the title of his book, *Why Am I Afraid to Tell You Who I Am?* "I am afraid to tell you who I am because, if I tell you who I am you may not like who I am, and it's all that I have."[2] This question and answer acknowledges the assumption that rejection is a possibility, and if it occurs you will have nowhere else to go in that relationship. Therefore, a marriage that is becoming defensive is one where there is a growing fear of rejection.

If someone is afraid of being rejected, the logical thing most people do is to work at being accepted. In early childhood, we learn that doing what others expected was a very reliable source of acceptance. However, one thing was wrong. You were accepted and received approval only as long as you kept it up. From making your bed each morning to getting good grades in school, you learned what it took to form and maintain relationships.

This same basis for relationships often continues from childhood into your adult world and the marriage relationship. If your acceptance only comes from earning it, you keep doing more and more until you get tired. Weighing the need for continuing the relationship against your fatigue, you will either risk the loss of the relationship by stopping all those efforts or you will press on in a constant state of fatigue.

There is a solution. Let me point it out:

But now God has shown us a different way to heaven—not by "being good enough" and trying to keep his laws, but by a new way (though not new, really, for the Scriptures told about it long ago). Now God says he will accept and acquit us—declare us "not guilty"—if we trust Jesus Christ to take away our sins. And we all can be saved in this same way, by coming to Christ, no matter *who we are or what we have been like* [italics mine].[3]

Here God sets forth not only the plan for eternal life, but also a model for us to follow in our marriage—a model of unconditional acceptance. In following God's example of accepting us unconditionally, we are told to reach out to our marriage partners with understanding and accept them with their strengths and weaknesses—the good and the bad—just as we promised on our wedding day. Then neither we nor our partners fear, for we are accepting each other in the same fashion as we are accepted by God, who created us and loved us first.

Summary

Some Christian marriages fail because the partners, in forgetting God accepts them as they are, cease to accept one another in the same manner. Thus, the partners put each other on a performance or "please me" trip, which all but promises an early end to their relationship.

6

Twice They Were Strangers

"I don't even know you." The words echoed down the clinic corridor as the lady rushed out of my office in tears. She stormed down the stairs and out into the parking lot. In her outburst she was not referring to someone she had never met, but rather to her husband who was still sitting stunned in my office.

"I guess we *are* strangers," he muttered as he searched his pocket for the keys to his car.

Although they still lived together, they had come in separate cars—one more evidence of the growing apartness that had been coming on for years.

"I'll call you if anything changes," he said, as he left to follow his wife's trail to the parking lot.

As I watched out the window I saw him pause for a moment, searching the lot for her car. She had already gone. Like a person with no place to go, he slowly got into his car and drove away alone. I never heard from either of them again.

At one time in the past, all married persons were strangers with each other. Then they met and began to date. In their growing to know each other better a courtship developed, they became engaged, and finally they married. What some people fail to realize is that growing to know each other does not end with the wedding; rather, it continues throughout the marriage.

As I mentioned in the previous chapter, some married people never really get to know each other at all. Even though they are married, they remain strangers because they only share a *part* of themselves with their spouse.

But far more painful to behold are those husbands and wives who were very close and intimate in the early years of marriage, but now have grown apart to become *strangers for the second time*. Only those who have experienced it can really know this lonely hurt as they remember the way they were. It *was* so good.

Becoming strangers in a marriage can be compared to the spread of a malignant cancer. It continues to grow, snuffing more and more life from the relationship until it ends in death by divorce. As I mentioned earlier, you experience all the same emotions as if someone close to you had died. Some have even said it is worse, because physical death is definite. In the death of a relationship it keeps coming back to life, only to die again and again.

An early sign of estrangement is when personal needs are being met more and more outside of the marriage. In a predictable manner the couple begin to turn away from each other to new sources of support. The needs that were met by the marital partner are now being satisfied somewhere else. In the initial stages it can be very subtle. Examine your motivation if you seem to have a growing need to spend more time with friends, your job, church committees, or even your children at the expense of time with your partner.

I see people turning elsewhere because it simply feels good for them. Their basic needs of loving and feeling worthwhile are once again being satisfied, but by someone other than their marriage partner.

In group therapy I recently observed a new couple who

appeared content and well adjusted on the surface, but underneath there was a subtle emptiness that kept eating away at my diagnostic mind. (I usually feel unsettled until I can really put my finger on why a couple is in therapy. Often the reason they state and the real reason are different. This was one of those situations.)

I listened intently as they praised each other on how well they carried out the separate tasks in which each of them were heavily involved. Having been married for over twenty years, the husband related how his wife had been a model mother. She had put her children ahead of everything else.

In similar fashion, she praised her husband's dedication to his work, which she said consumed most of his time. He was very successful. His total commitment to his job had moved him nicely up the ladder of promotions and pay raises. Providing well materially for his family helped remove any guilt.

Suddenly it hit me. Listening to them elaborate on all the responsibilities each of them was so totally committed to, I noticed that neither had included their marriage on the list. *They were staying busy to avoid each other!*

Furthermore, as dedicated Christians they had developed excellent "spiritual" sources for getting the personal recognition they needed. Let's face it: we all need personal recognition. The problem comes in the source of this acknowledgment. If more and more of it comes from outside the marriage, the marriage will definitely weaken.

The difficult task ahead for this couple was to give up their established "substitute" sources to return to the unestablished source of their marriage for their recognition and support. Both had agreed they were close at the beginning of their marriage. But back then, before children and vocational success came, all they had was each other.

Another sign in this malignant process of turning outside your marriage to meet your needs is when one spouse *overly encourages* this for the other. This happens when both seem more interested in having their own needs met than meeting the needs of their partner. By encouraging your spouse to meet more and more of his needs outside the marriage, the pressure is taken off you to meet them in the marriage.

At this point let me say I realize not all of your needs will be met in your marriage. This would be placing unrealistic expectations on that relationship. Nor am I saying you should not be committed to your job, your children, your church, or other important tasks outside the marriage. To reemphasize, the problems come when these activities and the resulting relationships *replace* the marriage in importance as the source for feeling worthwhile and loved. Even once the outside sources are recognized, it is difficult to lower their priority to once again make room for the marriage.

A sign that indicates your marriage is definitely failing is when you find you are becoming increasingly uncomfortable when alone with your spouse. In response to this feeling you will find yourself becoming more involved in activities and situations that take you away from your partner. More and more of your time will be spent with others. Even if you are with your spouse, other couples will probably be present.

Friends are great. Every couple needs them to complement their marriage. Later I will discuss in more detail the vital importance of outside support and guidance to the marriage relationship. The trouble in outside sources comes when you find that you must have others around all the time in order to feel comfortable with your mate. Intimacy is then on the way out.

Can husbands and wives who have become strangers ever be best friends again? Is there a way to treat the failing marriage that is close to dying? Can there be an alternative to divorce or continuing to live within a sick marriage? Yes! Let me show you how.

First of all you need to *decide* you are going to rebuild the relationship rather then end it. Without this decision nothing really will happen. When you make that determination to stay married and work on it, you need to know that (1) it is God's will and (2) that the process is usually slow and difficult. Some couples who have gone through it have referred to the pace as "growth by inches." At times it is so gradual that they are certain nothing is happening.

Although growth is slow, it usually is very real. You will recognize that aliveness does come back as you rebuild your lines of communication. Once again you will begin to see signs of life in your marriage. By life, I mean experiencing those good, warm feelings *from the marriage relationship* rather than from substitute sources outside the marriage.

As your marriage comes back to life, so do you. The process of deterioration that has been destroying your union is reversed. The desire to give to each other once again becomes basic in the marriage.

Let me make one more point on the challenge of your rebuilding. Although counseling is helpful and even necessary for many in achieving this change, I am the first to admit that not all couples need outside help to do it. However, *everyone* working on resolving their marital problems, whether they are in counseling or not, will be required to face the *test of patience* while the relationship heals and begins to grow again. One consolation to remember is that it also took time for the marriage to break down in the first place.

To rebuild your marriage you must go back to the basics of relationships. Remember that all relationships, including your marriage, are formed and maintained by the voluntary desire of each person to meet the needs of the other. Create a setting whereby your partner cannot help but respond to you. For instance, suppose you would like more attention from your wife in the evenings. Rather than demanding it, start doing the supper dishes, putting the children to bed, or doing any other task that routinely takes her away from you at that time. Wives, if you would like more of your husband's attention on Saturday afternoon, start cutting the grass for him or clean up the family car so that this time is free for both of you together. You may have better ideas, more suitable for you. But find a way to meet each other's needs in your marriage.

In answer to my question "What advice would you give to Christian couples with marital problems?" one evangelical leader, who is himself dealing with such problems, told me: "You must learn that the feelings of romance in a marriage *follow* the acts of love—doing loving things. When we begin to do the right, loving thing toward those who we are commanded to love (whether we feel like it or not) God compensates by giving the *feelings*."

In order to meet each other's needs, you must first know what they are. This will often create an immediate risk of being vulnerable due to the possibility of rejection if your needs are ignored. Revealing your needs only to have them rejected is fertile ground for emotional hurt. Consequently, before anyone will divulge their most intimate needs they must sense a security, so that the risk is tolerable.

There are definite steps to rebuilding your marriage

relationship. They include *commitment, revealing needs,* and *adjustment.* Commitment must come first. Revealing your needs will follow. Then adjustment will enter the rebuilding process. As each step begins, the others keep working. Therefore, when the rebuilding process is operating in full force, all three steps are functioning together like a synchronized team.

Commitment means you accept your partner unconditionally and that you will always be there *no matter what.* It is the absence of rejection. Commitment, so to speak, is taking your hands off the doorknob to the back door of your marriage. You will find that commitment and risk-taking grow simultaneously as your marriage is tested by more and more openness. However, until your unconditional promise of commitment is established you cannot proceed in rebuilding. This must be your decision, and it must come before the other steps.

Inherent in your commitment is your willingness to let go of the bad feelings and memories from your marital past. I am referring here to those events that initially created distrust and caused your needs to go unmet. Regardless of whether you or your spouse were responsible for them, *now* both of you must let go of them.

No matter how difficult it may seem to be, keeping at the rebuilding process is a growth factor in itself. Even though nothing may seem to be happening, *the commitment not to quit* reflects a belief and confidence in the future of the marriage. This also implies an acceptance of the other person and the marriage as a whole.

At one time I was seeing an insecure young couple in a therapy group. Week after week they kept telling us they were not going to continue coming, and that divorce was a serious alternative to solving their problems. Somehow they did not quit coming, but they returned each week with the same tale: this session would probably be their last.

Then one night, in distinct contrast to other evenings, they looked much better to everyone. They were relaxed and discussed with confidence some of their unsolved problems. Sensing the improvement, one of the members asked if their marriage was better.

"Not really," replied the wife. "We still have all our problems, and our communication is as lousy as ever."

The session continued and nothing more was said about it until the end, when one of the other members asked them the question that had become routine, "Will we see you next week?"

To everyone's surprise they said, "Yes, we have decided to definitely give this a try." Commitment to the group and to each other was established. Progress followed closely. Incidentally, the group's acceptance of them also took one giant step forward.

Revealing Needs. Once there is evidence of a commitment, risks lessen and each spouse can begin to reveal more of his personal needs to the other. These needs will vary from mowing the lawn and cleaning the house to sitting together under the stars sharing some of your innermost thoughts and feelings. Realize that *all* of your needs are important—both the practical and the emotional. Actually they are all interrelated.

Realize that *your* needs are unique to you. Only you know what they are; therefore, only you can adequately communicate them to your spouse. Too often we expect our partner to know what they are without revealing them.

It is very easy to hide your personal needs behind critical statements pertaining to your spouse's behavior. In this situation, all that is usually heard is the criticism. So instead of responding to the need, the tendency is to defend one's self.

Let me illustrate. Suppose you need to sit alone with your spouse in the yard after the children are in bed. The critical statement would be, "You never sit with me in the yard after we have the kids in bed." (Incidentally, the words "never" and "always" are deadly words that raise our defensiveness and are certain to start a fight or stop communication.)

Focusing more on the need than the criticism, the same message would be, "One of the nicest times of the day for me is when we can sit alone in the back yard after the kids are in bed. Even though we seldom do it, I really need that time alone with you."

Analyze how you would have responded to these two very different messages.

Obviously, the second statement is better. It does not criticize the partner but rather gives that person room to respond voluntarily to the need. *Do not tell your spouse what to do; rather, state what you need.*

Adjustment. If relationships are built and maintained on meeting one another's needs, then it is not enough just to know what those needs are. You must respond to them. This is where adjustment comes in—that fundamental thread that runs through all relationships.

The strength of any relationship is centered on each partner's willingness and ability to make changes in themselves for the purpose of meeting the other person's needs. If you are sensitive and flexible to your spouse's needs, the relationship grows. On the other hand, if you are rigid and uncompromising, the relationship will wither and die.

To truly understand adjustment you must be able to clearly differentiate between the *willingness to change* and the *ability to change*. They are often erroneously considered the same, feeding unwarranted hostility in a relationship. The motivation to change is often questioned if one feels his spouse is *unwilling* to change, when in reality he may be *unable*. If a desired change is not occurring in your marriage, determine for yourself whether your spouse is truly unwilling or rather unable to effectively make that change. Mistaking one for the other becomes extremely frustrating for both partners.

This "willing" and "able" distinction was made vividly clear to me by a couple I was seeing at a rural medical clinic where I consulted once a week. They were a German farm couple with not much room in their lifestyle for feelings. Only one thing was important for them: *work!*

During one of our sessions the wife told me her husband never said, "I love you." She went on to say that she would like to have him do this, "just like the neighbor's husband tells his wife."

My logical question, of course, to the husband was, "Do you love your wife?"

I knew the challenge ahead of me when he replied, "I'm here, ain't I?"

When I asked him if he would be willing to start telling her that he loved her, he replied, "I suppose I could. But the words tend to stick in my throat. I never heard my folks say it to each other, nor did anyone tell it to me when I was growing up."

As our session continued I learned that during the winter months, part of his daily routine was to get up before his wife every morning, put on the coffee, brush the snow from her car, and start the engine. Then when she was ready to leave for work, her car was nicely warmed.

She had a factory job ten miles away, which helped out financially during the slim winter months.

"Do you enjoy getting up and doing this each morning?" I asked.

"I hate it!" was his immediate reply. "The only person in the world I would do that for is sitting right there," he said, pointing his finger at his wife. "I know she likes that done for her," he concluded.

At that very moment she and I simultaneously realized that that was his "I love you." He would have been *willing* to say the words, but he did not have the *ability* to convey it verbally as sincerely as he did with his actions.

Once your partner knows your needs there must be the freedom to meet them in his or her own unique way. Only then is it sincere and real.

Adjusting to one another's needs does not come automatically. Three important ingredients are involved, and they all must work together as a unit.

First you must *know yourself.* To be able to adjust and make effective changes you must be in touch with who you are. Get a realistic hold of your strengths and weaknesses. Clarify in your mind your likes and dislikes. Knowing yourself well is essential, for adjustment entails making changes in one's self for the benefit of the partner.

Secondly, you must *understand your spouse.* Try to successfully understand your partner without cluttering the understanding with your personal judgments and opinions. At this point try to remain objective. Ask what it is that is "real." Put meaning behind your spouse's feelings and behavior. To the best of your ability, try to determine their cause and effect.

Once you *understand* these needs, even though you may not agree with all of them, adjustment will be easier and more effective. Realize that understanding your partner's feelings and behavior does not necessarily mean you agree. These two *different ideas* are often confused as meaning the same.

Thirdly, to successfully adjust to your partner you must *be skillful in communicating.* Communication is extremely powerful in the success of any relationship. Do not underestimate it! The problem most often mentioned to me by couples seeking counseling is, "We can't communicate." On the other hand those couples who improve inevitably tell me, "Now we can talk."

My next chapter concerns communication.

Summary

Another cause for Christian marriages' failing today is the absence of front-end commitment, and an insensitivity to each other's needs of loving and feeling worthwhile. In desperation people are turning to sources outside of the marriage for their recognition and merit, and the marriage dies.

7

Talking Back: Communication

The actual *experience* of communicating is as significant as the words that are spoken. In a unique way, the process of communication feeds a relationship. Like anything else that requires nourishment, your marriage must be fed regularly and adequately if it is to be properly sustained.

In this short chapter I want to discuss with you how to communicate. If what I say appears to be basic, that is because it *is*. If it seems repetitious because you have heard it somewhere before, most likely you have. But if you are tempted to skim over it because it is familiar, please avoid the temptation. As simple as these truths may be, I find that many Christian marriages falter and die because the partners do not communicate with each other. So whether this is new material or review, I say, *"Read on!"*

Communication is a skill that is learned. If at this time you feel you are not good at communicating, fear not: *you can learn*. Most of us have learned through a combination of experiences reflective of our individual family backgrounds. However, if you need to learn now, you can be helped through reading or attending seminars and classes.

But above all you learn by practicing. Make yourself do it even though it seems awkward. Practice communicating, especially to your spouse, and you will improve. I have seen it happen time and time again.

Now let me give you some pointers. Obviously, what I am about to say does not include all the skills and tools of communication. Rather, I have selected a few areas that seem to have the greatest importance in improving marital communication.

1. *How a message is said is as important in most cases as the message itself.* Give thought not only to the words you choose, but also the tone of voice, your physical gestures, body language, and other nonverbal tools that help you communicate. King Solomon said, "A soft answer turneth away wrath: but grievous words stir up anger."[1] Remember, it is often the actions accompanying the words that make you message effective.

2. *Be sensitive to timing.* The effectiveness of most messages is also directly related to *when* they are spoken. Often that precise "right" moment can never be repeated. Nothing can replace that missed moment in your marriage. It is gone forever. Frequently, our attention to our personal convenience dulls our sensitivity to the power of timing in communication.

3. *Learn the importance of silence.* Communicating a message at the right time also implies knowing when *not* to say it. Your silence can be one of the most powerful of all your communication tools. Used effectively, it can say a lot. This was demonstrated over and over again in Jesus' ministry, especially while He was standing trial the night before His crucifixion. There are times to speak and there

are times not to speak. Learn when *not saying it* says it best.

4. *Be a sensitive, perceptive listener.* When communication fails, the most frequent problem is that of not *listening*, rather than not *talking*. A skillful communicator does not contaminate what is being heard by his personal thoughts or feelings. How often have you heard only part of a message because instead of listening you were already thinking about what you would be saying in response? Good communication begins with listening. Look what Scripture tells us on this subject: "Dear brothers, don't ever forget that it is best to *listen much, speak little,* and not become angry."[2]

A skillful listener knows listening is done with more than just your ears. You also listen with your eyes and your intuitive feelings. *Listening with your eyes* means being sensitive to the nonverbal messages your spouse is sending. Watch the person's eyes. They are windows to that person's feelings. With practice you can learn to read in your mate's eyes joy, fear, happiness, guilt, anger, and other emotions. When you or your partner are uncomfortable about your relationship, eye contact will be avoided. On the other hand, when eye contact is established easily, the relationship is unquestionably growing more intimate. Has not even our Lord promised, "I will guide thee with mine eye"?[3]

You can also pick up other nonverbal messages expressed through body language and behavior. For example, a man I was seeing told me he was not nervous during our sessions. Yet his restless fingering of a button on his coat told me otherwise. Learn to listen with your eyes. What you see is often more important than what you hear.

Talking Back: Communication

5. *Listen to your feelings.* Some call this intuitiveness; others refer to it as "gut feelings." While you are listening to the words your partner is saying, ask yourself what you are feeling and why. The answer will help you understand the full message and its meaning.

Practice and develop your communication skills. Be aware that you express thoughts, feelings, and expectations and that you have a wide variety of methods from which to choose. Remember that communication involves listening as well as talking. Being an effective listener not only will give you a better understanding of what is being said, but it will also show your partner you are genuinely interested and that you truly care.

As you can see, communicating and adjusting are not simple tasks. A commitment and determined effort are required from *both* of you. However, in so doing you will become very close to your lifetime partner, so close that you cannot possibly imagine you were ever strangers.

I was recently reminded of this in two similar, yet very different, situations.

The wedding was over and we were waiting our turn to offer best wishes to the new bride and groom as they stood in the receiving line. They had both been students in my marriage and family class at the college. As a matter of fact, they met each other on the first day of class.

As Judy and I approached them, the bouyant young groom said, "Hi, Professor Dahl. Can you believe it? Just a year and a half ago we enrolled in your class as total strangers. Now look at us. It's hard to recall a time when we didn't know each other. It seems like we have always been together."

As I shook his hand and kissed the bride (which Judy

will agree is one of my favorite things to do at weddings), I thought, ''Just like all of us. These two people now deeply in love were total strangers once.''

As we were driving home my mind was reliving that moment at the reception. I found myself comparing it to an experience I had at the clinic. I was receiving warm appreciation from a couple who were falling back in love and starting a new life. They had just completed their long and painful journey through counseling to rebuild their marriage, which had almost ended in divorce.

''We will never forget our first session over a year ago in your office. Although we had been married for over fifteen years, we had become absolute strangers. Now look at us; we are not only still husband and wife, but we have become best friends.''

Whether you are strangers once like the newlyweds or strangers twice like this couple, learn to be strangers no longer.

Summary

Another factor in why marriages in general fall apart is the oft-repeated reason of failure to communicate. A Christian person can, in the power of the Holy Spirit, *will* to communicate with the other partner in marriage. Do it!

8

From the Saturday Night Mistress to the Sunday Morning Saint

A midsummer night's dream is a rare occurrence almost anywhere, but especially in Minnesota. A night last June was one of those times. It was an ideal night, one that is indeed a dream six months later as we watch the snow moved about by the sub-zero winds over the still, frozen ground. But tonight it was June, not December, and the setting was idyllic. The moon was full, softly lighting the patio and yard, yet casting shadows and creating forms that added mystery to the evening. There was a warm southerly breeze, the usual Minnesota chill totally absent from it. Best of all, there were no mosquitoes.

It had been the usual busy Saturday, filled with errands and chores. Now the children were bathed and in bed, ready for Sunday school and church the next morning. Even though my wife and I had said nothing to each other, our minds were running on the same track. Showered and in my pajamas, I started for the bedroom when Judy said, "Go on downstairs; I'll meet you on the patio in a few minutes." I spun around faster than a quarterback giving a handoff on a play up the middle of the line and disappeared out the patio doors.

Strategically arranging two chairs in just the right places by the patio table, I sat down and waited to see what would happen next. Suddenly I seemed to forget I had been married for eighteen years and was the father of three children who were asleep inside. Rather, I had the feeling I was rendezvousing with my mistress. I slid down in my chair, gazing off into the sky trying to absorb and feel all that was happening around me. The words of Psalm 8 came to my mind as I looked up at the stars. "When I consider thy heavens, the work of thy fingers, the moon and the stars, which thou hast ordained. . . . O Lord our Lord, how excellent is thy name in all the earth!"[1]

The silence of the evening was interrupted by the patio doors opening and closing. Looking up, I saw Judy standing in the moonlight with her sheer negligee flowing in the evening breeze. She was holding a tray of cheeses and fruits that were delivered before me with a warm kiss and a gentle "I love you." Although the tray of hors d'oeuvres was a labor of love, I found myself initially ignoring them, for I was totally captivated by this woman standing before me. I could not take my eyes off her as I found myself magnetized to her beauty. She let her body talk to me as I reached out to touch her to be sure she was real.

Responding to my gentle tug, she sat down beside me. Together we started feeding each other fruit, pieces of cheese, and kisses. We ate, talked, and touched as time seemed to stand still. There is always something very exhilarating about being together outside. My eyes continued to drink in her beauty as the moonlight danced on her soft tanned skin. Even the breeze cooperated by momentarily exposing hidden parts of her body, only to cover them again. Tonight was one of those special nights God gives us from time to time to experience the deep love we have for each other.

From the Saturday Night Mistress to the Sunday Morning Saint

As our evening together continued our feelings for each other heightened. We were both deeply aware of how much we were in love. I never dreamed I could love anyone as much as I loved her just at that moment. The moon passed behind a cloud, and like an orchestra moving into the next movement of the symphony, Judy suggested we go up to bed. With my arm around her I left that enchanting place, thanking God for this woman He had given to be my wife and for all the love we experience together. I was deeply in love with my "Saturday night mistress," but best of all, she was also my wife.

I was awakened by the sun hitting me in the face and a voice from the kitchen yelling, "Get up, we're already ten minutes late." Stumbling out of bed, my mind still sleeping, I realized vaguely that it was morning—not just any morning, but Sunday morning. My trip to the bathroom and on to the kitchen for breakfast was interrupted by the verbal reminder to shine my sons' shoes. I arrived at the breakfast table after everyone was nearly finished.

Part of the challenge of Sunday morning breakfast is to consume it in record time without suffering from indigestion during Sunday school. My wife kept issuing the orders as the rest of us responded as a somewhat unsynchronized team, colliding as we gathered up Bibles, offering money, and a hairbrush.

As I backed out of the driveway, Judy reminded me that we had forgotten our son's Sunday school workbook. Realizing that I would not win the debate as to whether or not he really needed it that day, I obediently pulled back in and rushed in the house to get it.

Now we were fifteen minutes late. Thankfully, Sunday morning is one time when few cars are on the freeway, allowing me to make record driving time to church.

Under my wife's direction we got into our respective Sunday school classes out of breath but on time. My mind still racing from the short but hectic morning, I found it difficult to concentrate on the lesson. Judy's pinches on my leg, coupled with her subtle pointing to the correct verse when it was my turn to read, kept me on the track and concealed quite well my preoccupation with other thoughts. Without a doubt she was in control.

The hour passed and class was over. We started the next race—talking to everyone in the hallway long enough to be courteous while getting the kids to the restrooms and then upstairs to the sanctuary before the choir marched in. (We make it about half of the time. The other times we slip in the side door after the invocation.)

As we settled in for the morning worship service, Judy quietly leaned over to whisper that the pastor wanted to see me sometime. I wondered for a moment why he had not said something directly to me after Sunday school since we were in the same class, but I thought nothing more of it. I tried to concentrate on the sermon, but for some reason I was as restless as my two sons sitting on either side of me. Several times my wife had to remind all three of us to sit still. Part of my "problem," of course, was that I was still reliving the night before.

Judy continued to do her best to keep me in the service by finding the correct page for the hymns, opening the Bible to the Scripture passage being read, and commenting to me throughout the sermon, "Wasn't that a good point the pastor just made?" When it comes to entering into the worship service, compared to the rest of the family she indeed appeared to be the "saint."

Following the benediction we once again started our trek through the crowds to make our way to the car. As usual, we all got separated talking to different individuals.

(Incidentally, the warmth and fellowship that comes from talking to various people in our church family following the service is one of the highlights of the morning for me. I wish there were some way open fellowship could be developed more into our regular services.)

Twenty minutes after the closing note on the organ, I finally made it to the car only to see that everyone else in the family had arrived ahead of me. Judy was sitting in the front seat, her door open while she visited with the pastor and his wife, who were standing next to the car.

This is when I really blew it.

Concerned that I had kept everyone else in the family waiting, and totally forgetting that the pastor had wanted to talk to me, I courteously but briefly greeted him as I got into the car, started the engine and said, "Let's be going!" I quickly pulled away from the church and started home. Tense from the hurry of the past few hours, as well as the fact that the children were tired and hungry, I drove home in a somewhat detached state of mind.

What I did not realize was that my wife was very quiet as well. That is unusual for her after a Sunday morning at church. As we were heading down the freeway, she broke the silence by commenting that I had certainly been cool and aloof to the pastor; furthermore, it had embarrassed her. That is when I remembered he had wanted to talk to me. I quickly rationalized that he could have said something. Her retort was that I had not given him a chance. We were starting a fight.

I looked over at Judy and observed her rigid disapproval of my behavior. Listening to my feelings at that moment, I thought, "I do not even like her." I later learned she had the same dislike for me at that time. She was tense, rigid, controlling, trying to be sure we all did what was right when we were around church. Her motives were right and her intentions good, but I didn't like the way she was doing it, and my reaction toward her actions was extremely negative.

Both of us sat silently for a moment, not sure where the conversation was heading. Then it hit me.

"I don't believe it!" I said.

"Believe what?" she replied.

"How totally opposite my feelings for one person can be in less than twelve hours," I answered.

She knew exactly what I was talking about. Together we began to notice how our responses sometimes vary so dramatically with each other's behavior. Last night I told her she was my "Saturday night mistress." She filled me with love and emotion and I fell off to sleep thanking God for her and her love. Today she became a "Sunday morning saint," once again trying to do what was best and right for everyone. But I find I want to avoid and ignore this person.

"Which one really is the godly woman?" I asked myself. I was thanking God for one and evading the other.

We learned several things from this experience. First of all we realized in our own marriage how important it is to openly talk out the feeling reactions we have to each other's behavior. Our Sunday afternoon was saved because we were able to talk about the morning on the way home. How important it is to be able to deal with your feelings and talk to your partner about them as soon as you become aware of them.

The other lesson for us—and for all marriage relationships—is that when one of the partners becomes more rigid and controlling, it often has a negative effect upon the other. Although a disciplined control is good at times in our lives, expressing this between partners in a marriage usually has a negative effect. As some of my couples have said during therapy, "No one wants to be married to a critical parent."

What my wife was trying to do that Sunday morning was indeed good. What she was doing was for my benefit and favorable appearance to others. This is why it can become doubly confusing—one spouse is trying to do what is best for the other and it is not appreciated. Our experience has helped us not to feel so responsible for one another's behavior. In other words, if I do not know which verse to read when it is my turn in the Sunday school class, it is my problem, not hers.

By the way, now that she is not keeping track for me I feel I have to pay closer attention myself. This rigid control of one spouse by the other is more common in evangelical marriages than in others. If you find that you dread your Sunday mornings or any other times, examine your marriage relationship. Maybe one of you is trying more than necessary to run the other spouse.

There is an epilogue to this twenty-four-hour saga, by the way. It is now Monday morning and I am back at the clinic. After finishing my second appointment, my secretary informed me that the next appointment just canceled. Having a free hour and having an office only five minutes from home, I decided to take the opportunity to sneak home for a surprise midmorning coffee break. The timing was perfect.

As I came in the back door Judy was just stepping out of the shower. Greeting me at the bedroom door, soaking wet, she threw her arms around me and whispered in my ear, "Your mistress is back."

I never did try to explain to my staff why I was wearing a different suit when I returned to work that morning.

Summary

Some Christian marriages have gotten into trouble when one partner feels overly responsible for the other's behavior and comes across as too sanctimonious or "proper" and the offended partner fails to confront the problem on the spot by honestly talking it out. Learn to be righteous without being rigid, helpful without being domineering.

9

The Double Bind

Ambivalence is defined as a situation in which you are experiencing conflicting pulls. Some call it being placed in a "double bind."

The frustration of millions of Americans today, especially evangelical Christians, is directly related to their realization that they are in the middle of situations where they are being pulled in two or more directions. Both may be good in themselves, but they are pulling in opposite ways. Responding to one pull causes you to become more distant to the other. This is one of the most common causes for stress as people face the daily task of deciding which way to go.

Marriage is directly affected by this phenomenon and is usually one of the "pulls" in that conflict. There can be a variety of forces pulling at the marriage. When you sort them out, however, they all seem to fall under two main categories: *time* and *money*.

When a new marriage crisis is presented to me at the clinic, a frequent complaint from a spouse is, "I am sick and tired of being third or fourth on his list of priorities." This person is saying she is tired of time, money, or some other interest winning out over the marriage in this perpetual struggle.

"How can all this good be bad?" was the question asked in frustration by a diligent Christian businessman I had been seeing. He presented convincing arguments why it was necessary for him to continue in each of his responsibilities. Yes, he convinced me that they all were very good in themselves, but each one took him away from time with his wife, and now he was beginning to see that what appeared initially to be *good* was in reality *bad.*

Today we are living in a time-drained society. Everyone is busy, never having enough time to do the things they really want to do. For evangelical Christians this presents special problems. Involvement in a church schedule will cost them a major portion of their nonworking time each week if they truly attempt to keep up with it. On the other hand, if they do not keep up with this schedule they will often experience guilt and a sense of not doing what is expected.

The "faithful evangelical church member" spends an enormous amount of time each week at the church. Each Sunday alone, the average church member spends four and a half to five hours in church, assuming he attends Sunday school and both the morning and evening services. Of course, preparation time at home, plus commuting, is extra. Any church committee meetings scheduled before or after the services add to the time. The end result is that a major portion of your "day of rest" is spent very actively in the church program, often away from your family.

But the demand of time does not end on Sunday. Everyone is also expected to attend the midweek prayer service, which in the eyes of many pastors is used as a barometer to measure the "spirituality" of the members. (By the way, when was the last time you spent a significant amount of time in prayer at the Wednesday night prayer meeting?)

In addition to these regular weekly services are the one or two evenings a week for those special programs that desperately need you: choir practice, youth meetings, women's guild, men's brotherhood, and other church committees. In addition, you may meet a couple of times a month for early morning breakfast meetings. What a great day it will be when the Christian church returns to the New Testament concept of *caring* for its people (thankfully, there are some who do), instead of putting demand upon demand on them in order to sustain a program.

I challenge you to make out a list of the church services and activities you are *expected* to attend each week. Next to the activity, place the estimated amount of time required and total the hours. Next, superimpose this schedule onto your work schedule and the hours required each week in your employment. Add the hours in the twenty-four-hour day given to sleep. Now, how much time is left for your family? After that, determine how much time is left just for your marriage? You can now begin to understand the *double bind* you are in when it comes to time.

Over an extended period of time, this kind of schedule has some very interesting psychological effects. You become accustomed to being tired, and with the tiredness varying degrees of hostility and frustration set in. You are careful not to let these emotions show to anyone, especially around the church.

In time, you will recognize your tiredness and frustration as evidences of your excellent involvement in all these "necessary" church activities. You will consider having no time for yourself, your marriage, or your family evidence of your sacrificial commitment to the program.

What happens is that you become comfortable only when you are uncomfortable (tired and frustrated).

Once in a while, through no choice of his own, some faithful Christian brother who has been in this time trap for years comes out of it. Through an unlikely turn of events he finds himself off all committees. Consequently he is not busy and he becomes rested, feeling exceptionally good both physically and emotionally because he has time for himself. But can he enjoy it? No! There is now a new twist that keeps him from the joy and happiness the Lord has provided for him.

When you are exhausted, frustrated, and even depressed over an extended period of time, you will find it a real problem to once again enjoy feeling good, even though you are rested and have some time for yourself and your marriage. These good feelings are new and therefore strange to you. A new set of feelings is difficult to accept, even when they are better than the old ones.

Rather than just accept and enjoy the good feelings, many Christians encounter a new problem. Due to their previous conditioning, feeling rested implies they are not busy and that means they are not a good worker. This introduces guilt. The guilty person says, "I feel rested and have time; therefore I must not be carrying my share of the load."

This is exactly the psychological *double bind* where many Christians find themselves. Are you one of them? Are you either rested and guilty, or busy and tired? Either way you lose! You are in a trap whereby you cannot truly feel *good*.

This *double bind* was never God's program for your Christian life, or for your marriage. I am convinced that being caught in this losing predicament is a major weapon Satan uses to shoot down the joyful Christian and destroy the Christian marriage.

The Double Bind

Evangelical churches today are filled with husbands and wives in this condition. Not only do they not know how to get out of it, they do not even know they are in it! It can be a deception of the first order. I know people who do not feel good about all the good they are trying to do. It's chaos! Take a close look at not only what is happening to you, but also to your relationships—especially your marriage.

As I mentioned earlier, the other force that has a major control on our lives is money. This is partly true because of the time required to earn it. But it goes further.

Following a recent group therapy session I co-led with a psychiatrist friend, I learned an important lesson about money. We were desperately trying to figure out the significance of one group member's behavior. Each week he would go on and on about how frustrated he was, living with a roommate he could not tolerate. Yet to the group's dismay, he would never do anything to change his situation, and he became very angry whenever anyone would suggest he move out.

Finally, one bit of very significant information was revealed to us. This person was paying a token rent to the other person who owned the house and apparently didn't need the money.

After attempting to arrive at a profound psychological reason as to why this person would continue to put up with such an unhappy situation, my psychiatrist friend sighed and said, "I guess we will have to write it off to the 'first law.' "

"What's that?" I asked curiously.

Realizing that he had one on me, he said, "You mean to tell me that with all your professional education you don't know about the 'first law'?"

Shaking my head in ignorance, I knew he was going to

get as much mileage as possible out of this "rare opportunity."

In a low voice, imitating a professor emeritus filled with wisdom, he said, "Sit back and sharpen your mind to receive one of those great pearls of wisdom that will transform the very fiber of your being." He warned me that once I became enlightened to this law I would see it working again and again in people's behavior.

"The law will never leave you," was his solemn warning.

At that point I felt he was getting a little overdramatic. But you know, now I have to admit he was *right!* Over and over again this law comes back to me, flashing like a neon light in my head as I observe people. The law has often explained to me why people form relationships with certain other people. It also has given me answers as to why people spend their time in the manner they do. (It's as Ed McMahon would say on the *Tonight Show:* "All you ever wanted to know about life, *everything* you will ever need to explain why people do what they do, is all wrapped up in this one little law!"

Now that my life has been changed by knowing this secret law, I will pass it on to you—all at no extra charge. The first law, according to my psychiatrist friend, is that *the flow of money governs all behavior.* That is all there is to it. Although it is not very long or complicated, I find it is disgustingly true. In essence, what this law says is that people's behavior is based largely upon whether they will get paid for it or whether it will cost them something. Money is at the basis of their behavior.

Of course, Scripture is in touch with the first law as it points out the futility of money as the basis for your happiness.

The Double Bind

He who loves money shall never have enough. The foolishness of thinking that wealth brings happiness! The more you have, the more you spend, right up to the limits of your income, so what is the advantage of wealth—except perhaps to watch it as it runs through your fingers! The man who works hard sleeps well whether he eats little or much, but the rich must worry and suffer insomnia.[1]

For the contemporary evangelical there is often a sense of guilt related to having money and a feeling of virtue connected to living in poverty. Actually this virtue may be more of a rationalization by the poor to help them accept their poverty more easily. The problem, however, is not in having money, but the stress involved in obtaining it.

The first step toward sin is to spend time obtaining money at the expense of time spent building those relationships that are more important to us, starting with our walk with God. In the same way your marriage is affected by the love of money. Relationships suffer when they are neglected, and spending time earning money is one of the most common ways of neglecting your marriage.

On the other hand, if God has allowed you to be blessed with money and you have it in its proper place in importance in your life, thank Him for it. Be good stewards, liberal givers, and enjoy it!

There is a price attached to getting out of this *double bind.* Whether it is time, money, or some other force that is drawing you away from your marriage, to change it will cost you something. Are you willing to pay the price? One thing I should point out here is that if you choose to leave things as they are, there is also a price for that, and it will be far more costly.

For example, *Time* magazine recently reported: "Pelé, Brazilian soccer hero, was separated from his wife Rose after twelve years of marriage and three children. His life has been filled with various commitments, including soccer camps and TV commercials that keep the retired soccer star on the road. Said Pelé, 'I have been on the road for 22 years. Rose says it has to stop, *but I cannot* [italics mine].' "[2]

After reading this, I am sure your mind runs to others closer to home in the same situation but with different demands—pastors and other evangelical leaders.

In a recent study on divorce reported by the *Minneapolis Star,* we learn that the parsonage is increasingly becoming "a place of marital conflict." Along with other reasons, the report attributed much of the marital breakdown to three essential parts of what they refer to as the "clergy mystic." These are: (1) high expectations of congregations, (2) fear of failure, and (3) the *time* they are expected to spend on church business.[3] Pastors, like everyone else, can get caught in this time trap.

As you can see, if you choose not to get out of this double bind, there is still a high price to pay. It can cost you your marriage.

Marriages often receive merely the scraps of time left from your schedules after everything else is done. One reason for this is that you live under the illusion that you are spending more time together than you really are, simply because you live under the same roof. Seeing each other only early in the morning and late in the evening is not enough to keep your marriage alive. In the morning we are preoccupied with the events that lie ahead for the day, and by evening we are tired and need to wind down. Whether we have been working outside or inside the home, our best time has been spent.

You must realize that to begin giving time to your marriage you must take time from some other area of your life. This area you will drop out of your schedule may be one you really enjoy, one that satisfies a great many of those needs that were previously not being met in your marriage.

Now the pressure is really on. What will you give up? Can you cut down on your over involvement in church without feeling guilty? Which Christian organization board will you turn down to spend more time with your spouse? What about that hunting or fishing trip you planned? Will the women's club survive without your leadership? Are you willing to accept the cold rejection that may follow when you say no to that important position no one else can do as well?

How much money are you willing to give up earning in order to spend more time with your spouse? Will you decline that promotion because it requires more travel time? I beg you to make the correct choice; only *you* can do it.

Let me tell you about one man who was faced with this problem and made his choice. Six months ago a veteran police officer and his wife came to me for counseling.

"I have had it!" she said angrily as she related the years she had felt like a widow. While her husband had been a "good" police officer, putting in his long hours serving the community, she was on her way toward getting a divorce.

For six years her husband had been a police sergeant, which gave him status, signified by the stripes on his uniform, and an extra $300 a month in salary. The catch was that during the entire six-year period he was required to work the night shift while his wife worked days on her job. They only saw each other on weekends, and then the tension was so thick you could cut it with a knife.

Before I could even suggest it, the husband told me he was giving up his sergeant's rank. This would shorten his hours and put him on a daytime shift.

"No amount of money is worth what that job is costing my marriage," he said. This man considered the price and chose to pay it. Today they are happy and $300 a month poorer—or are they really richer?

Everyone's price is different. Only you know what it will cost you to change. Just remember there is a greater cost if you choose not to change.

Here are some tested tools that will help you in your effort to get out of the double bind.

1. Determine before God that you are ready to make whatever changes are necessary, and trust Him to lead you in knowing what they are.

2. Establish your priority list. Let your spouse and children know what these priorities are. Live by them consistently.

3. In the area of relationship priorities I believe they should come in the following order:

   a. First and foremost, give top priority to your spiritual relationship with God. Be firmly in touch with His will for your life, and follow it.
   b. Your relationship with your marital partner comes next, and should receive the love, attention, care, and concern reserved for this most important human relationship.
   c. Next come your children. After your spouse, your children's needs must receive your attention as their parent and the one responsible for their care.
   d. Vocational and employment responsibilities are next. Although your career is often placed first in your life, it really belongs fourth—below the others listed ahead of it.

(Following these four main relationship priorities will come others unique to your individual lives. Please note that this list is arranged in this fashion because you must have a solid relationship with God before you can effectively relate to your spouse. In turn you cannot adequately care for your children if your marriage is not in the right place. Likewise, your effectiveness on the job is directly related to the happiness and stability of your family life.)

4. Husbands and wives, discuss your finances and determine how important money is to both of you. Be honest. Often this area is never discussed between spouses. Determine together the relationship between the amount of money you need and the amount of time you are both willing to give to earn it. Then make some decisions about time and money in your marriage.

5. In the same manner, discuss together your time schedules. Rearrange them in such a way as to allow time to be alone individually with your children, and time alone as a couple. Then carefully protect this schedule so that outside influences do not erode it.

6. In the area of time, here are some specific concrete suggestions that have proven successful to other couples. Perhaps they will also be helpful to you.

   a. Have at least one night a week as family night. Let absolutely nothing interfere with this time that has been set aside for your spouse and children. Some families vary the night from week to week. Be flexible.

   b. One night a week have dinner alone *as a couple*. Alternate between going out and staying at home, depending upon your mood and the cash available at the time. If you choose to eat at home, make it pleasant with china, candles, music and other things to set the atmosphere. No matter what you have on the menu, it doesn't cost any more to make it nice *just for the two of you.*

c. Wives, arrange to meet your husband regularly for a noon lunch or dinner on his turf. Especially if you are a house-wife, get a babysitter and meet your husband at his office and go to lunch at one of his usual restaurants. This will allow you to become a little more acquainted with his world.

d. At least three or four times a year, leave your children and get away as a couple even for a weekend. Place yourself in a setting where for a brief time you are away from your children, telephones, and all the other demands that con-sistently come between you and the one you married. Devote this time to recharging your marriage.

(I have given you five concrete suggestions that other couples have found extremely helpful to their marriages. Now, realizing that every marriage relationship is unique, let me suggest you add a few more of your own.)

e.

f.

g.

h.

i.

Summary

Many evangelical marriages are failing today because couples have fallen into the *double bind* of giving in to the pressures of time, money, and other forces at the expense of their marriage relationship. Reevaluate and then rear-range your priorities.

10

Every Married Person Needs an Affair

He traded in the station wagon for a sports car. The bald spot on his head was covered with a new hair piece, and he wore new tinted glasses. Some of his best friends did not recognize him. Fashionable, more expensive designer clothes replaced the usual drab suits he had worn for years. In addition to these not-so-subtle changes, he had become increasingly quiet and withdrawn around home. These changes had been happening for quite some time, but everyone was too busy to notice.

Then it finally hit. He told his wife he had been very unhappy and needed to get away for awhile to think, to spend some time alone. He rented a "modest apartment" on the other side of town. The address and telephone number remained secret because he needed to get away from everything, including her. But she could call him at the office.

Later she learned that the modest apartment was really a bachelor's pad, lavishly furnished in a style that was totally opposite from the conservative furnishings in their home.

Although no one had said anything yet, his friends and business associates were noticing that he had lost interest in a business that had totally consumed his attention for years. Getting new clients was no longer important, and that was a change. He was coming to work later, leaving earlier, and his noon lunches were lasting up to two hours. In the past it was often customary for him to remain at the office and eat a bag lunch or have something sent in from the local sandwich shop.

Although all the evidence pointed toward it, no one really wanted to believe what was so contrary to the image he had portrayed for all these years. But it was true; he was having an affair.

He stumbled over his words as he tried to explain to his wife how he and this young girl had become such good friends. Even though she was young enough to be his daughter, he talked about her maturity and sensitivity to his needs.

"We enjoyed talking to each other and never expected it to be more than that," he continued.

He never did describe their arrangement as an affair. Usually no one involved really does. Like the others, he said, "Ours is something different." He called it a "special friendship" or any other number of neutral labels, rather than facing up to what it really was: an affair, a relationship of infidelity.

Completely stunned by the revelation, his wife could not think at first. She was in shock. Every possible emotion rushed through her at lightning pace. Confusion was followed by anger, then sorrow. Thinking it over, compassion came for her husband and the confusion he must be experiencing. Then she was back to sheer anger again. Over and over her mind flip-flopped as she tried to assimilate what was taking place.

Every Married Person Needs an Affair

This story is not unique. It happens more often than most of us realize. The story is usually the same—only the name, age, business, and denomination vary. The story is the same even though everyone who has an affair claims theirs is different. It is happening all around you, yes, even to Christians.

Who is the person who has an affair? What is he like? Contrary to what you may think, many are not basically immoral, irresponsible persons who are living a carefree lifestyle of satisfying their sensual desires. Actually, they are most often the opposite.

This person is a solid, conservative, family man. He is a leader in the community, serving committees and organizations that benefit all. He has his own business or holds a prominent position in his company. This person is the epitome of dependability, very conscientious in all that he does. He has worked hard all his life, sacrificing himself for the good of others. He is basically a dedicated man.

If he is an evangelical he is usually active in his church, holding at one time or another almost all the leadership positions. He is the last person in the world most people would suspect. "Who would have believed it?" is the question that comes when the truth emerges.

For those who fall into an affair of this type, it is usually the first time it has happened to him. In the past, he was the one who was especially critical of others in similar situations. But now it has happened to him. Why? What brought it about?

"Why did you do it?" is another question always asked. Although there are almost as many answers to that question as persons who ask it, I believe there are some basic reasons common to most affairs.

In understanding why they do it, consider where this person is coming from. Whether it is the husband or the wife, for years they have conscientiously denied their own needs and the needs of the marriage for other things. For years they have been busy doing for others, receiving the usual praise that reinforces their lifestyle and forces them even deeper into that behavior. Doing for others is good, but if it gets out of balance you are in trouble.

His day is usually spent building his business, which requires long hours and sometimes pays very little. In the evenings he meets with committees and organizations as he does his share in the church and community. The few hours he has at home are consumed with such things as Little League, picking up the dry cleaning, and cutting the grass. The occasional afternoon of golf or a fishing trip is received with protest from his wife. She in turn is on her own treadmill, caring for the children and running the household. Both of them are tied down, involved in everything but themselves and their marriage. The feelings of love and romance that existed in the beginning are not there now. The turnoff comes gradually due to repeated rejection. Then finally the day comes when you think those feelings are dead. No thought is given to them anymore because you assume that part of your life is definitely past.

But it is not. If those needs are not being met, you are vulnerable and can fall into the clutches of an experience you will later pay for dearly. Most people who have this type of an affair do not consciously go out looking for it. They just don't stop the affair when they see it coming. The longer they wait, the more difficult it is to stop.

One day it could happen to you. No one is immune. The setting and circumstances may vary, but the process is the same. Check out your feelings as you see how it happened to one person. His story is true.

Every Married Person Needs an Affair

"I was pleasantly surprised when she brought in that hot cup of coffee late in the afternoon, especially when I hadn't asked for it. She must have known it had been an especially long day for me, and it wasn't over yet. The report I was working on was full of corrections and it was too late to have it retyped that afternoon.

"It was already six and only a couple of office staff were still around. Somehow she knew I wanted to work further on the report; she offered to stay late and retype it if I could drop her off at her apartment. Her friend, who had driven that day, was ready to leave now and couldn't wait. I was more than happy to return the favor to get the freshly typed report. It was only a mile or two out of my way, and I had nothing special planned that night at home.

"Finishing the report, I quickly packed my briefcase and together we closed up the office. The empty corridor echoed from our footsteps as we laughed and chatted on our way toward the parking ramp. Although I had been exhausted most of the day, I didn't feel tired now. I couldn't figure out when this surge of energy had come, but it really felt good.

"She seemed so vibrant and alive. I had forgotten how, when you are young and single, you can turn off the cares of the job when you walk out the door at night. It was apparent that she could do it, and it had a contagious effect on me. For a moment I forgot I was a vice-president facing a tough board meeting the next day. I also forgot I had a wife and three children at home, one who had been running a fever when I left this morning. I forgot it all for the moment.

"Following her instructions, I turned right as we pulled out of the ramp and headed down the boulevard. Even that was a change. For years the car had automatically turned to the left, taking the usual route home. She snapped on the radio, turning it to her favorite station, and started to sing along with the music. Although I didn't know the words, I found myself humming and tapping the steering wheel right along with the rhythm.

"Turning left off the boulevard, we proceeded around a little park, past a shopping center, and into a modest complex of apartment buildings. She pointed to her building, and I pulled up in front. We sat for a moment looking into each other's eyes. It was one of those uncomfortable times when it seemed that each of us was waiting for the other to speak. I broke the silence by thanking her for what she had done for me that night. She thought I meant the report, and so did I. But in reality I knew later it was for what I had felt that evening with her.

"Driving away, I continued to leave the radio tuned to the same station, filling the car with her music. I now realize I was trying to make the feelings last as long as possible. Why, I hadn't felt this way in years. I was excited, happy, alive, and young again. These feelings really felt good, but they were frightening because they were so strong. The thought that this was wrong entered my head for only a moment. Then it left as I rationalized: How could feeling so good be wrong?

"As I drove into our neighborhood, reality started to settle in. The rows of large, expensive houses with their carefully manicured lawns stood as monuments of judgment to our great professional success. They were too perfect to be homes. There was also a competitive conformity that no one ever admitted mattered to them. Waving to a couple of neighbors from my open car window, I quickly changed the radio station. I was now embarrassed at the music still playing and didn't want them to hear it.

"I met my wife pulling out of the driveway as I drove in.

She smiled and I waved. She was late for her women's auxiliary, and this year she was president.

"The last of my good feelings left me as I entered my monument and sat down alone at the table for dinner. Everyone else had gone to one thing or another, except my oldest son who was still in bed with a slight fever. In her usual thoughtful way, my wife had kept dinner warm in the oven for me.

"Next to my plate was the customary note from my wife with a list of things that needed my attention while she was gone. She is a strong, well-organized woman whom I respect very much. Yes, I do respect and admire her, but any other feelings are pretty much dead.

"Following dinner, after checking on my son who was sleeping and doing the tasks on my list, I settled into my chair to study the freshly typed report for tomorrow's meeting. I knew I was in trouble as I tried to concentrate on the contents but found myself thinking instead of the person who had typed it. The feelings were back, and I wanted to see her."

He told me that this is how the whole thing started. He never had any intention of having an affair, but he did. The seed of desire was planted and one thing led to another. There were more late afternoon cups of coffee and reports to be typed at the last minute. This meant more trips by her apartment and eventually invitations to come in. Then there were picnics and lunches in rendezvous places. Notes and glances were discreetly exchanged in the office. Then the bubble broke. She wanted to know when he intended to tell his wife and get a divorce. She wanted to tell her friends about her plans for marriage.

He didn't have to tell his wife, for she already suspected something. Finally she confronted him. This time she had not wanted to follow her usual reliable instincts. Being an honest man, he admitted the whole thing, almost relieved to do so. His wife was hurt, but what really shook her up was the fact that he wasn't sure he wanted to give up the affair.

This "in love" feeling is what confuses everyone, especially the persons involved in the affair. The feeling is so strong that even after the infidelity is discovered they may still want to continue the extramarital relationship in spite of the cost to themselves and others.

How often the innocent party will ask me, "How can my spouse possibly feel he is in love when he barely knows the person?" Usually affairs happen quickly. My answer to them is that they are not "in love" with the *person,* but rather with that *feeling* they haven't experienced for years.

This is borne out as I listen to them tell me about the new relationship. He does not talk much about the person, but goes on and on about how he feels when he is with her. Any reference to the person is usually connected to that wonderful feeling he gets when they are together.

It is not the person he is reluctant to give up. What he really doesn't want to give up are those feelings—that experience of being alive and finding the excitement of love again.

Sitting in my office, this man told me he had never been so confused in all his life. Being an executive, he had always been good at making decisions; this time he could not seem to do it. He looked at me and said, "I hadn't felt so good in years, yet now I feel good and bad. I'm confused! Why does an affair have to be so bad when it makes you feel so good?"

He almost fell off his chair when I told him I thought every married person ought to have an affair. From the shocked look on his face I was sure he was preparing himself to hear some type of open-marriage solution to their problem. What I told them was very different, but it is the solution to an extramarital affair with its powerful, potentially destructive force. Affairs are deceptive. They destroy individuals, careers, certainly marriages, and families. Anyone close to the person involved in an affair is affected.

I point out that the problems arise when people have affairs with the wrong person. Have an affair, but have it with your spouse. Create the situations to give you the good feelings, but let your husband or wife be that partner. This removes the conflict that leads to destruction from the experience and allows the good feelings to remain. An extramarital affair is wrong because it is sin. It produces infidelity, adultery, and lies. No amount of rationalization can change what God says: "Honor your marriage and its vows, and be pure; for God will surely punish all those who are immoral or commit adultery."[1]

The benefit of an affair is the change in lifestyle from our overemphasis on the rigid controls and expectations of others to becoming more sensitive to our own emotional needs. You have every right to feel young and alive again. Just find it with your spouse, not someone else. Then you have these feelings guilt-free and with God's blessings. Also, some very interesting changes often happen to your spouse. I know several who have done so, including this man and his wife.

She made a decision to love him back into the marriage, and it worked. The Bible has told us that love is even greater than faith and hope. "There are three things that remain—faith, hope, and love—and the greatest of these is love."[2] When you are confused and don't know what to do, try loving. You can't go wrong. But you must stick with it.

In loving this man back into the marriage, his wife

realized that some changes needed to be made on her part. She abandoned the usual list that accompanied his evening meal. She turned some of the women's auxiliary duties over to her assistant chairman and began meeting her husband downtown frequently after work for dinner. Sometimes they never made it home, but ended their evening by staying overnight at a hotel. To his amazement he began feeling alive, but this time with his wife. Best of all there was no sin, no lies, no infidelity, and no guilt.

Later his wife confessed that in all honesty his affair with the secretary had in some ways helped their marriage and had helped her as an individual. She made it clear that it was still wrong and she would not wish it on anyone, not even her worst enemy. But it did force them to look at their life together and get straight what is really important. Spending a night at a hotel is far more fun than attending every auxiliary meeting. Her parting comment to me was, "I just wish all married couples could learn what we did, *without* the affair and pain that accompanied it."

Summary

The lesson to be learned from this couple and others who have experienced affairs is that when basic needs go unmet, you are vulnerable for an affair. Often, if you are a conscientious person you will routinely set these needs aside because they appear selfish or self-centered. Please, do not ignore them in yourself or your spouse. If they go unattended they may very well surface impulsively, but powerfully, in a relationship with someone other than your spouse. You can stop that from happening by having an affair . . . with the person you married.

11

The "Submissive" Husband

"I just don't understand all this women's liberation business everyone is talking about." The words tumbled out of his mouth as he plunked himself down in my office beside his wife. "The other day she called me a male chauvinist, and I don't even know what that word means."

He told me that he couldn't get his wife to do a thing since she recently took that "assertiveness training" course. With a deep sigh he shook his head and said, "My Mom always let Dad be the boss and they got along just fine. Why can't we?"

I knew exactly why this couple was in my office, and I hadn't even had the opportunity to say hello yet. Everything came out in the first moments of our session.

Some people find that just walking into a counselor's office triggers a relief valve. Here was a confused, frustrated husband who had no idea what his role was in the marriage anymore. His wife was also apparently carrying on a search for herself in the same area.

Wherever you look today you will find couples who are confused about their marriage roles. We no longer have a clear definition as to who does what or who is who in the marriage relationship. The necessity of two incomes, modern household conveniences, and day-care centers for the children are just a few of the numerous reasons why there is a growing vagueness in the definition of the husband and wife roles in many homes.

The debate over who is going to do a specific chore often turns into a power struggle that can grow to the point of threatening the existence of the marriage. I have seen it happen frequently. Many factors contribute to the "who's boss at our house" debate that has fueled heated discussions from sophisticated college classrooms to casual social groups.

Even though the Bible clearly teaches an equality between men and women, it also gives an order of authority for the family. As we all know, that order places the husband at the top as the person primarily responsible to God for his family. The wife is under him in the family, and next come the children.

However, in spite of all the books, seminars, and papers written on this subject by theologians and other qualified (and some probably unqualified) Bible scholars, there is still much confusion and debate over this issue in many marriages. Frequently I have asked myself what it is that causes so many couples to continue to parade into my office with unsettled ideas about their roles in marriage. In all of their discussions there definitely is something missing. What is it?

We discuss the fact that husbands should love their wives as Christ loved the church. We also examine the meaning of submissiveness and how the wife should be this way. But it seldom seems to happen just by discussing and agreeing to it in theory.

Then one day I got a clue. A husband with whom I was counseling said, "If I am in charge, I expect my family to accept my word as final." The words, "I am in charge" stuck with me as I pondered their situation even after they left my office.

Finally it came to me. We live under a false assumption that the counterpart of submissiveness is dominance. If the wife is to be submissive to her husband, then logically it will follow that he is to be dominant over her. Theoretically this is correct. He is the one primarily responsible to God for the members of his family. However, preoccupation with his dominance can subtly lead him away from the realization that he is to be submissive to God.

The confusion comes when we start in the middle of the process, focusing somewhere in the area of the submissive wife or the husband's love for her. These are important, but neither are starting points.

The key is a submissive husband, a man who recognizes that just as his wife is under him in the family, likewise he is under God. His focus is not on his wife's position in the family but rather on his own. This is where it all must begin. Husbands, you must place yourself directly under the lordship of Jesus Christ and be obedient to His will. Look to God first; then see the effect it will have upon your marriage and family.

Actually, submissiveness is the hallmark of the victorious Christian. It is a quality in the believer that has confounded the unbeliever throughout the ages. The committed Christian has always been the epitome of strength, daily submitting himself to others in obedience to the will of God.

Jesus sets the example in His ministry. From the humbling experience of washing the apostles' feet on the evening of Passover to His submission to the authorities later that night, He obediently followed the will of His Father in heaven.

This was not an easy task even for Him to do. In His

prayer earlier that evening, Jesus revealed some of His humanness as He asked God to get Him out of what was in store for Him, if it was God's will. "He walked away, perhaps a stone's throw, and knelt down and prayed this prayer: 'Father, if you are willing, please take away this cup of horror from me. But *I want your will, not mine* [italics mine].' "[1] Our Lord was totally submissive. In spite of His power as the Son of God, who is eternally co-equal with the Father, He continued in this stance of servanthood throughout the trial to His ultimate death on the cross.

As in your Christian life, your marriage is also affected by this submission to God. Place your life squarely under the authority of your Heavenly Father. Make Jesus your Lord as well as your Savior. Take this Psalm at face value and see what happens: "Commit your way to the Lord: trust in him, and he will act."[2]

When a husband gets hold of the true meaning of submission by committing his way to the Lord, an exciting cause-and-effect process is placed into motion that will bring joy and happiness to the entire family. And why shouldn't it happen, when it is part of God's perfect plan for you?

By submitting, you husbands are consciously and actively seeking God's will for your lives. In doing this you will open yourselves to receive and experience the fullness of God's total love for you. As His love fills and indwells you, you will find you simply cannot contain all of it. This love will run out of you and into your wives. It is here that you will discover you are loving your wives as Christ loved the church, and it will seem like you are doing it without even trying.

When God's love gets hold of you, as it will from your active submission to His will, you will find yourself compelled to love others—especially your wife. It is totally impossible to contain all the love that is poured out to you from your Heavenly Father.

The next step is the transformation you will see in your wife. As she receives your full and unconditional love, something very beautiful will be happening inside of her. She will grow in beauty and become alive again.

Just as you are compelled to love her as a result of what is happening inside of you, so also she will find she is compelled to be submissive to you because of what is happening inside of her. It is her natural response to your love, not a reluctant response to your demand.

I will always remember that young progressive, independent-thinking wife who told her husband, in my presence, that under no condition would she ever let herself get into that old-fashioned "submissive position" with him. "The submissive wife is outdated," was her belief. Several weeks later her husband did something that totally thrilled her, and through it she experienced how deeply he loved her.

He then asked if she would do something for him. I cannot even remember what the request was, but I will never forget her response to his question.

Still caught up in the thrill of her husband's love, she jumped up and threw her arms around him and lovingly said, "Darling, there isn't anything I wouldn't do for you!" Immediately all three of us realized what had just happened. She had placed herself in a totally submissive role to her husband without even trying. It was simply her natural response to his love.

Later she told me she realized that her submissiveness was a compelling force from within her.

"You cannot help but want to give of yourself com

pletely to someone who totally loves you as you are," she told me.

Her submissiveness did not begin with a response to a command; rather, it was a natural response to her husband's love, which must come first just as Christ first loved the church.

I am convinced that the inner beauty of a married woman is directly related to the quality of love and caring she receives from her husband. She definitely is a product of his love for her. As God's love passes through him and into her, a transformation is taking place in her. When the wife begins to show a warm, submissive response to her husband it will have the same positive effect on him. It really becomes a glorious circle spiraling upward in an exciting, beautiful way.

In turn, your children will receive a solid foundation for their own growth. You will be excellent models whereby they can build their own healthy patterns of behavior. They will see in you and experience in themselves the results of wise leadership, the rewards of submissiveness, and the power of love in your home.

There is one other aspect of submissiveness that most men totally miss. Husbands are to also be submissive *to their wives*. It goes in both directions: first to God, but also to the wife. "Honor Christ by submitting to each other."[3]

This is often missed because men inaccurately regard submissiveness and weakness as synonymous, and they see weakness as unattractive.

Men tend to live by the myth that they are attractive to women primarily because of their strength, confidence, and independence, which is all wrapped in a package called masculinity. But in reality the opposite is true.

Women are attracted to men not because of their strength, but because of their vulnerability. Take a look at the plots of literally scores of love stories. Predictably, in the end the woman leaves the strong, successful man who does not need her to go away with the weaker one who does. These stories are built on a true principle.

It is man's vulnerability and weakness that attract women to them, because *women have a greater need to be needed than to have their own needs met.*

Recently this was vividly illustrated in group therapy as I listened to a woman go on and on about all her needs her husband was not meeting for her. He, in turn, was telling the group how very hard he had been trying. Back and forth their discussion went. Nothing seemed to be happening.

Then, somewhere in the process of a session, he began to open up with some of his true feelings. The more he talked the more emotional he became. Tears came to his eyes and his voice was shaky. As the group became intensely focused on what was happening to him, I also noticed a change in his wife. She sat there silently and took his hand. Her attention, along with the others, was totally captured by him. Without any reservation she willingly set aside her needs for his. Why? The answer is obvious. She was needed by him and that is always more important.

Every man has his area of vulnerability. The problem is that men have been conditioned more than women not to show it. He will try to take care of everyone else, demonstrating his strength and masculinity. His needs and weaknesses are securely sealed off in the privacy of his personality. Early in his childhood they were placed there as he learned that the expression of fear and other similar emotions are a weakness. The message to the little boy with tears in his eyes is, "Wipe away your tears. Men don't cry." Obediently, he wipes them away, but not just for that time. He wipes them away forever.

Expression of fear and other emotions is not a weakness. Actually, the opposite is true. It takes strength to let someone see where you are vulnerable. In the marriage this is all wrapped up in a submissiveness that the husband needs to show to his wife.

The weak person will take the easy way out and continue to hide his feelings in the safety of his mind. It takes courage, trust, and a whole lot of strength to be submissive to your wife by letting your vulnerability show. In doing so, however, you will be telling her in the most genuine way possible that you need her, and that will make you very attractive to her.

Take the risk. Be a submissive husband. Submit yourself to God and start that beautiful chain of events that will give you immeasurable joy in your marriage. Then submit yourself to your wife by revealing your vulnerability to her.

Submission is not a sign of weakness; rather it is your strength.

Summary

Many evangelical marriages are failing today because Christian men do not truly understand the meaning of submission. They focus on their dominant role in the home over their wives rather than on their own submission to Jesus Christ as Lord. Furthermore, they see submission as a weakness, not as an act of Christian obedience. Submission starts with the husband and carries on to the wife and the children.

12

Security for Your Marriage

Go back with me to that time when you and your spouse first met and started dating. As you fell in love and the relationship moved closer toward marriage, remember how everyone seemed to get into the act? Especially if your chosen partner met everyone's approval, friends, parents, relatives, church members, and anyone else around rushed to give their support and encouragement to the budding new lovers.

"Aren't they a cute couple? They seem to be so much in love," people whispered behind your backs but loudly enough so you would be sure to hear. The support intensified as the eventual wedding day became more of a reality. Everyone smiled and gave their nods of approval as you walked by.

Whenever Mom went shopping she purchased two of whatever was on sale. After all, she knew "the kids" could use one to set up housekeeping. Showers were given. Plans were made. The one hundred and one details that required attention were efficiently cared for by the massive team of people who just automatically seemed to come together to pull this whole thing off. At that time it seemed as if the whole world revolved around these two who would be married soon. Absolutely nothing could interfere with the activities involved in planning the wedding. They came first.

The security was great. There was really nothing to worry about because someone else was taking care of everything. If some task did happen to fall on your shoulders, you had plenty of help from others. No one turned you down, whatever the request might have been. Friends and family were all around you. They needed to be a part of your wedding. Nothing bad could happen. You were in secure hands and it felt good.

No one could have received more encouragement from friends and family than Judy and I. The fact that her father had been the pastor of our church automatically gave us an edge on receiving support from the entire congregation. Six weeks prior to our wedding he died unexpectedly. This generated additional support from everyone around. People cared and they showed it. They could not seem to do enough for us.

Even Judy's boss quietly passed a wadded bill into the palm of my hand during a handshake. It was obvious to me that he didn't want Judy or any of the others standing around to know what he had done. He whispered, "Have an evening out on me." Later, when I unwrapped the bill and saw that it was a twenty, I knew we would have at least two nights out (remember, it was 1960!) with some left over.

All this support and security continued to build to that exciting climactic point, the wedding.

Although we didn't realize it at the time, the wedding was a beginning for us but a culmination for everyone else. They had accomplished their mission and now could return to their day-to-day routine. Life would go on as usual for everyone but us, the newlyweds.

We were in for the shock of our lives. The realization of really being on our own had not yet hit us. Riding high on the enthusiasm of the celebration of our wedding night, we left on our honeymoon.

A dramatic emptiness hit us as we returned. Ten days earlier we had left a church and parsonage filled with food, flowers, laughter, and the gaiety of happy people celebrating our wedding. The memory of that night had continued throughout our honeymoon.

Now, tired from our trip yet excited over the anticipation of being home, we pulled in late at the parsonage. Both of us looked for the evidence of someone awaiting our return, but the house was dark and totally void of any signs of life. That was strange for the church parsonage. Speechless, we sat for a moment in our car just staring at the house. It had never looked so desolate to either of us.

Slowly we got out and walked in the back door. Although the house was dark, the silence was even worse. Our only greeting was a brief note taped to the opened door of an unplugged refrigerator. It told us that Judy's mother had gone to look for a house in the city where she would be moving. As we looked around, things were already packed in boxes ready for shipping. Although it had once been home, we felt now like we were walking into someone else's house.

Flopping a mattress over on the floor, we made a makeshift bed and comforted ourselves by the fact that tomorrow things would be better. We would drive on to my parents' home to celebrate the Fourth of July in a manner that has been tradition for as long as I can remember.

Morning came quickly and we could not seem to get out of that house soon enough. It was no longer home. As we drove away we saw the house merely as a place of memories. Our wedding day, ten days earlier, seemed like ancient history.

Needing to reclaim some of that enthusiasm and interest we had enjoyed so much before our wedding, I drove faster than usual to my little home town of Lyle. Even the short ten-mile trip over familiar roads to this little farming community seemed to take longer than usual.

A sense of happiness returned. We felt excitement in the air as we pulled into a town getting ready for its "celebration of the year."

At first the realization didn't hit us that the jubilation had nothing to do with our return. Our time had been two weeks earlier when we were married. That was past, and now the attention was on other things. Oh yes, everyone was moving about with a similar excitement and dedication. But this time it was for the parade on Main Street. My father happened to be in charge of it that year. Then there was the traditional picnic that was served on the front porch following the morning festivities. Everyone was busy, and this time we were in the way.

All the support and interest from our Christian community that had given us such a sense of security had somehow vanished. Before our wedding we had been the center of attention; now we seemed almost transparent as people walked by us. Sensing an abandonment, we silently thought to ourselves, "Where will we turn for our security?"

In one way or another this question is asked by almost every newlywed couple as they move from singleness into marriage. In contrast to the abundant support and interest generously given by the church prior to the wedding, the absence of response in the months that follow is a distinct letdown. Just when the new husband and wife seem to need this sustenance the most, they receive it the least. It is wrong to assume that the church is doing them a favor by leaving them alone. They need that continued acceptance and support as they adjust to being married.

Another time when the church seems to maintain a "safe" distance from its married couples is when they appear to be having marriage problems. The church often takes the stance that it is none of their business, that they should not interfere. Actually, the opposite is true. This is the time when the church should step in to perform its function of looking after the needs of *all* its members.

One Christian woman, whose husband became involved with another woman and ultimately left home, told me, "Living in the evangelical subculture produced certain standards of behavior and pressures that proscribed my wanting to be open with our problems. It was not spiritual to have a problem marriage. Since Fred and I were committed Christians and had chosen to serve God, I guess I thought the problems would magically disappear."

Then she went on to give some incredibly significant advice to Christians with rocky marriages: "I'd help them to realize that if they are having problems, they need the help and encouragement of the body of Christ. It's not likely they'll make it alone."

Notice how the apostle Paul instructs the early church:

There should be no division in the body; but . . . the members should have the same care one for another. And whether one member suffer, all the members suffer with it; or one member be honoured, all the members rejoice with it. Now ye are the body of Christ, and members in particular.[1]

As a husband and wife turn to each other to build or rebuild their marriage, they will realize that they must have support from outside their relationship. Their isolation must be broken. As one authority tells us, "It is simply not sensible to ask two people, usually young and inexperienced, to assume important and complex responsibilities without any resources or support. The family never before operated in splendid isolation, and in a time of great confusion it is even more vulnerable. But there is probably no way to increase support of the family and assistance to parents except in the renewal of community."[2]

Sociologists tell us that no man is an island. Neither are marriages. As a husband and wife need each other, together they also need a base of support outside of themselves whereby they can receive guidance, support, and a sense of belonging. For the evangelical Christian, this community or base must be the local church. The marriage must identify with and draw on that body of believers who are committed to one another through Christ's love and are living under the divine authority of God as He instituted it through His church.

Here and there throughout this book I have been especially hard on the church because I believed someone needed to say, "Back off and let people have some time at home." Please don't interpret this criticism to mean I believe the church is obsolete or unable to fulfill its ancient purpose of caring not only for the individual believers but also for its marriages.

The purpose of the church remains unchanged. Its power is still there. The problem is that the church has become silent. Its passiveness toward troubled Christian marriages reflects a definite neglect of the authority given to it by God to shepherd its marriages and families.

Sermons and seminars on marriage and family life are routinely included in church programs. I have personally had the privilege of being a part of several of them in churches in our area. But seminars are not enough. The church must go further. It must sense the responsibility to personally look after each individual marriage within its group of believers. If a marriage is left to its own support and control and it falters, there is no other place to turn.

Even back in the Old Testament the problems of marriages did not go unchecked or undisciplined. God simply did not let things go by the board; He instituted a government called Israel to look after the care and the discipline of His people.

Similarly, in the New Testament the Lord established a government here on earth through which His grace is fostered, His discipline carried out, His care exhibited, and His love made real. That government is present in His church. The place where marriages grow must be in the garden called the church.

The time has come to reinstate in the church the same kind of care and commitment for its members that was present when *Israel* walked with God, and throughout the history of the *church* when it walked with God. In 1 Corinthians, Paul gave explicit instructions on how the church should care not only for its people who had been divorced, widowed, or single, but also for its married people.

Today the evangelical churches are simply not looking after their couples. Like Judy and I, most couples experience a tremendous support system just prior to marriage, but it all closes down just afterwards.

On the brighter side, I have learned that in different places around the country some churches are regaining their vision to care for their marriages. In one particular church a situation arose where it was apparent to everyone that a certain couple was growing distant with one another. In response to this observation, two of the church elders got together with them. They confronted them with the fact that several in the church had noticed that their marriage had outwardly eroded. The way they had appeared for weeks in the services and elsewhere had caused everyone grave concern that their marriage was in difficulty.

Readily they admitted their problems to these two men who, as leaders in the church, had approached them with love and concern. (Contrary to what you may expect, I have learned from experience as a group therapist that direct confrontation coupled with love and honest concern will almost always bring a positive response from the couple. Remember, people want to be open if they know it is safe. In this situation the directness of the elders opened the door.)

These men continued to work with them, rebuilding a confidence in the love of their relationship. Continued support for their relationship was further assured as the elders told them that if there was ever a time they needed them, day or night, they were just a phone call away, even if it was three in the morning. The couple knew they meant it. Progress was made and the marriage did a complete turnabout. Remember, you can aggressively confront a couple when you are committed to stay by them as long as they need you.

When the leadership in the church personally takes responsibility or appoints someone in the membership to look after a troubled marriage within their fellowship, amazing things will happen. Not too long ago at a church in Ohio, the deacons asked a happily married couple in the church to look after a husband and wife whose marriage was in difficulty. The appointed couple were instructed to just sit and listen to the other couple once a week, trusting that through God's leading they would be given wisdom from the Lord to say and do things to enable the marriage to straighten out. Actually, benefits are realized by both couples as they go through an experience such as this. Several weeks later, it became evident that the Lord used this weekly session to put the troubled marriage back on the right track.

People caring for people is necessary to heal relationships. Consistently, the couples I see in group therapy do better than those who come in alone for office sessions. I believe the primary difference is that the presence of others gives care and support. A husband and wife will become strong as they draw sustenance from a base outside of their marriage. For the evangelical Christian, this base is the church. The church must once again become truly involved with the marriages in its fellowship.

I believe the educational programs for marriages and families should continue. Seminars on family life are an important part of the church program and reflect a very positive, healthy trend. But don't be deluded into believing that the discipleship of marriages ends there. That is just skimming the surface. It is the church's responsibility to literally look after the marriages of its people. This includes discipline and authoritative correction as well as love and nurture.

How to do it is the next issue. Like any relationship something must be done from both sides—the couple and the church. As in any relationship, the solution requires a consistent, sincere effort. It is not easy, but it can be done.

Let me speak first to the married couple. Whether or not you are having problems, plug in as quickly as possible to your church. Attend the services and fellowship with the members. Don't wait for them to reach out to you. Reach out to them.

If you are sensing problems in your marriage, I urge you

to drop the pride that has kept you from being open with others about it. After making it a matter of prayer, go to your church leadership with your need. Trust your pastor, deacon, or elder with your problems. God will in turn use the church to meet your needs in this area. This is His plan. In obedience to Him, turn to your church for help.

To the church leadership: Let me urge you to become bold again with the authority given you by God to guide and shepherd the marriages of your local church membership. Become actively involved in the care and guidance you are instructed by God to give as part of the function of the church body. You may do this personally or you may feel led to instruct another couple to help out with the troubled marriage, as was illustrated earlier.

If you sense that a couple is having problems and they do not come to you, go to them! It is your responsibility. This may mean putting yourself in an uncomfortable situation from time to time, but when it is done with love under the guidance of God, people will thank you. In most cases God will be able to work through you to save a marriage and family. Remember that these couples are part of your church family, and what you are doing *is* part of the function of the church.

The church's passiveness and neglect in this area have created a silence in response to the cries for help by evangelical marriages. Maybe our ears have been deaf to the cry. But now *listen* and you will *hear*. As you hear the cries for help, reach out in boldness, claiming the power given you by God through His Holy Spirit. As the Shepherd left the ninety and nine for the moment to go after the one lost sheep, let the church take the time and make the effort to reach out to the one lost marriage, rescuing it from destruction and divorce. Let us remain silent no longer.

Summary

An alarming reason for the failure of evangelical marriages is the church's silence concerning its ancient function of caring for its marriages. In turn, the couple with marriage problems has turned everywhere but to the church to seek help. The time has come for the church to aggressively return to its God-given role of disciplining the marriages of its members.

13

The Plus Element

Throughout this book we have looked at marriages. We have explored what they are and discussed what they can be. As you look around you the two visible extremes always stand out: good marriages and bad ones. But many are just average—neither good nor bad. They just go on day after day. You see them, but there is nothing that stands out as special. They are just . . . together.

Like your Christian walk, God designed marriage to be a beautiful, exciting experience that grows throughout your entire lifetime. Unfortunately, for many this never happens. Some marriages fail and end in divorce. Others fail but continue to exist legally.

Failing marriages are becoming more visible among Christians. We see an increasing number getting divorced. There is also that silent group who remain married, but endure an empty, frustrating, and totally unfulfilling relationship.

Are you in either of these groups? If you are like others I know, you watch the good marriages closely, secretly hoping to get some clues on how to make your marriage better. Looking over the masses of couples, every now and then you see one who has something special in their relationship. You envy it but can't seem to identify what it is. It has to do with the way they look at each other and the way they touch. A special awareness of each other seems to be present.

I believe these couples have really discovered the uniqueness of the marriage relationship. They know and experience the fulfillment God intended their union to have when He created it. Their marriages possess what I call the "plus element." This element is something extra that lifts their relationship above the mediocrity of the masses. Even though in today's society it is a rarity, in the beginning it was God's plan that all marriages have this quality.

As the plus element becomes a part of your marriage, you will notice some changes happening to both you and your marriage. There will be a sense of oneness, and you will not be able to conceive of being single again. As a matter of fact, you will have difficulty recalling that time in your life when you were alone and how it felt. Singleness as you previously experienced it will become totally foreign to you.

Often Judy will ask if I was having a rough time at a given hour of that day. When I discuss it with her, she inevitably replies that she felt it too, and sensed the need to pray for me then. Daily the awareness of your partner consciously comes to your mind over and over again, even though you are apart. Indeed, you are never alone.

Carefully studying our marriage as well as others who seem to have the "plus" element, I have discovered certain keys that can also put it into your marriage. Follow these seven keys and you will definitely begin to experience a warm, fulfilling marriage as God designed it to be for you.

1. *Relationships*. The first key in establishing the plus element is to recognize that your marriage is a relation-

ship. Furthermore, it is the most important relationship God has given to all married persons. Therefore, all the rules we have discussed in forming and maintaining relationships especially apply here. Your marriage deserves your very best in nurture and care. In return it will grow strong and not fail.

You are an important part of your marriage but not all of it. What is done and experienced by one affects the other. Your successes are shared by both; likewise your failures are shared by both. You are—together.

At the time you said your wedding vows God tied the knot creating your relationship and lifting it above you as an individual. *From then on the relationship must come before yourself.* It is something bigger than you alone.

2. *Giving.* Focus on your giving and the receiving will come automatically. When you are preoccupied with receiving from your partner, the result is a competitiveness that will definitely break down the marriage. Giving is the tangible evidence of your love. Giving and loving go hand in hand. One feeds the other.

Find a need and experience the joy of meeting it, expecting nothing in return. Oh, you will receive; but as I mentioned earlier, it will come as a natural response to your giving.

One afternoon I was scooping some ice cubes out of the freezer in the kitchen at our clinic to take home to make homemade ice cream. Our son, Peter, had just spent all his babysitting money to purchase an electric freezer for the family. We were excited about trying it for the first time. (Actually, in storage we had a hand-operated freezer that hadn't been used for years because we all are too lazy to turn the crank for forty-five minutes to an hour.)

While in the clinic kitchen I struck up a conversation with our cook. She told me she had been looking all over for a hand-operated freezer but could not find one. She explained that she needed one with a hand crank because she has nine grandchildren and for them the fun of making ice cream was for each to get a turn at the crank.

"I have one!" I told her.

"You do?" she replied, her eyes lighting up. "How much do you want for it?" she asked.

"I'll talk it over with my wife and let you know," I replied.

After returning to my office I telephoned Judy and said, "I've got a buyer for our old ice-cream freezer. How much shall we ask for it?"

After I explained who was interested in buying it, Judy came up with the perfect price. "Let's give it to her," she suggested.

We did, and I have heard many times how much she and her grandchildren have enjoyed homemade ice cream. Since then we constantly have been receiving corn, tomatoes, and other beautiful vegetables from her garden. Priced in the grocery store, the vegetables far exceeded the value of both the old and new freezer combined. I just wish I could find something else to give her!

This is a simple illustration of a truth that repeats itself over and over again, and it works best in your marriage. Giving is love made visible.

When you are faced with tension and problems in your marriage, try giving. If you will do it unconditionally and long enough, your partner will respond. The tension will leave and the problem will be solved or just go away. God has promised it.

3. *Adjustments.* The marriage relationship is dynamic. It is constantly changing. Recognize that there will always be highs and lows and that they are normal. The presence of highs and lows is *not* bad. *Expect* them. The important

thing is for you to be able to *adjust* to them. Remember the importance of adjusting to the challenges and stresses your marriage will encounter. The dynamics reflect that your marriage is vibrant and alive. To these changes your adjustment becomes a way of life and a key to the success of your marriage.

4. *Communication.* Always keep communicating. Daily let your spouse know your thoughts, feelings, needs, and expectations. Realize that communication is a skill that requires constant practice. It must be maintained and can always be improved. Most of all, remember that communication is the pipeline and what is said is the food that feeds your marriage relationship. If the pipeline is blocked and communication stops, the relationship will eventually starve and die. Through full and rich communication, the relationship will be nourished and will continue to grow strong and vibrant.

5. *Spontaneity.* In the marriage relationship there must be a time for impulsiveness, a time when your behavior is free from logic. Spontaneity encourages you and your spouse to do something for the sheer reason that you feel like it. When your marriage is filled with daily controls and responsibilities, an occasional moment when you give in to your impulsiveness together is like a breath of fresh air after being in a stuffy room.

I will never forget a certain Saturday afternoon when our children were younger. My wife and I seldom got out of the house together. There were several reasons, but the main one was that we couldn't afford babysitters. This afternoon we felt we did not have a choice: We had to go to a wedding. We didn't know the couple very well, but we were friends of the groom's parents. So we made the supreme sacrifice and hired a babysitter.

We parked the car, entered the church, and took our place in line waiting restlessly to sign the guest book. Judy and I looked at each other. We could read the other's mind without saying a word.

With a mischievous smile on my face I asked her, "Are you thinking what I am?"

She nodded, "Yes."

"You sign the guest book and I'll get the car," I said without a moment's hesitation. We missed the wedding and had one of the best afternoons of our lives.

Periodically, your marriage needs that breath of fresh air. Do something unplanned. Let go of logic and go with your feelings. Just be sure to do it together!

6. *Time.* Relationships are built on shared experiences, and experiences require time. There is absolutely nothing that can replace the spending of time together in your marriage. No gifts, favors, or anything can take the place of you.

As you spend time together, *create traditions.* Traditions are those times you spend together in some way that is uniquely yours. This will become especially significant as children become a part of your home. They will enter in and help create the tradition. No one really knows exactly how traditions start, but once you have one nothing can change it. It is done that way year after year. (By the way, this creates a sense of security for everyone.)

One of our family's traditions takes place in the celebrating of birthdays. Being too cheap to buy birthday cards, we have discovered the joy of creating our own. Peter, our oldest son, has always had an interest in drawing. In his typical grandiose fashion, he once made a large poster birthday card for his mother that covered the entire refrigerator door. Stephen, his younger brother, looking for the easiest way out, added his own greeting with a note and sketch on an empty corner of Peter's creation. All that was left was for Leah, our daughter, and myself to follow suit by joining in with our notes. This was the beginning of the family-birthday-card-on-the-refrigerator-door tradition. It now highlights each of our birthdays. The poster card gets photographed in colored prints and home movies. Our albums are filled with them. It remains on the refrigerator door for at least a week; no one dares to discard it!

A tradition is important not for the activity itself, but for the importance it signifies in the relationship. It is a special time when people feel they truly belong to each other.

7. *Christ-centeredness.* Center your marriage in Christ by committing your relationship to Him. As I mentioned under relationships, your marriage became an entity in itself when you were joined together. As you have committed your life personally to the Lord Jesus, do the same with your marriage. Together with your marital partner make the same commitment you did individually when you invited Christ to be Lord and Savior of your life. Turn your marriage over to Him and allow Him to protect and guide it. Once you have done so, daily acknowledge His presence through thanksgiving and prayer together. Remember, marriage is a model of our relationship with Christ.[1]

These are the seven keys. Perhaps there could be more, or maybe different terms. But whether you like the terms or not, please remember the truths they represent. That is what is important. If these keys become a part of your marriage, not only will the quality of the relationship grow, but it also will be guaranteed to be permanent. The possibility of divorce will be totally inconceivable.

The Plus Element

Do you remember when you were little and your shoes were always coming untied? Your mother probably taught you how to tie a double knot. This took just a little more effort and time than tying a single knot. Yet one thing is sure: It will not come untied.

There is another advantage in a double knot. Can you remember one of your friends pulling on one strand of your shoe lace? A single knot easily came untied. This was disturbing to me, especially before I had learned to tie my own shoelaces. One day my friend tried his usual stunt, but this time I had a double knot. Not only did the lace stay tied, but the knot became tighter.

Follow these seven keys of the "plus element" and you will tie a double knot in your marriage. Then not only will it stay tied, but also if someone tries to untie it your marriage relationship will respond by drawing more tightly together. May you and your spouse discover this permanent, beautiful relationship with each other.

Summary

Marriages with the "plus" element are characterized by
- partners who place their relationship above their own personal desires.
- the willingness of both partners to give each other what they need.
- the ability of both partners to adjust to changes and growth in the relationship.
- partners who will work at keeping lines of honest communication open.
- playful spontaneity
- the willingness of both partners to spend time specifically building and improving the relationship.
- partners who love Jesus Christ above all else.

14

Will It Ever Be
Like It Was?

There was warmth and happiness in their voices as they told me about the first years of their marriage. Those were good years. Everything had gone well and they had a great marriage. Their voices trailed off as their minds drifted silently into their own thoughts about the way they were. I chose not to interrupt the silence and break the spell of happiness they were privately enjoying as they relived some of their past.

Suddenly the stillness was broken, although there were no words. Her eyes started talking to me. They searched deeply into mine, looking for the answer first to see if the question should be asked. There was fear in her look. By now her husband had joined her. They were both thinking the same thought, even though neither spoke. Then the question had to be asked, "Will it ever be like it was?"

For those couples whose marriage was once good, yet now is in trouble, this question is always asked. They want some guarantee that the good they once experienced can be recaptured. Behind this question is the unspoken plea, "Reassure us that there is some possibility that our marriage will eventually get better." Everyone wants some type of hope.

As you have gone with me through this book and related it to your marriage, perhaps you are asking the same question. By now you have started to become acquainted with me. You know a little about how I think and feel. You have sat with me in the office, visited the college classroom, and looked in on my marriage.

I have not had the same opportunity with you, nor should I. I haven't been able to read your eyes or hear your words—but your spouse has. Therefore, take what I have shared with you and turn to each other for your answers. Find them within the privacy and the intimacy of your own marriage.

"Will it ever be like it was?" My answer for you is one that has been given to me from couples I have known—couples who have worked out their problems and rebuilt their marriages. "No, it will not be the same; but it can be better." You can never return to a stage in your relationship from the past. You must always go on.

But if you are having problems, it does not mean it will always be that way. If you are like many couples, you will find that your marriage can become better than it was. But you must honestly commit yourselves to each other and work on it or it will not happen.

The problems these couples encountered caused them to take an honest look at their marriage relationships and make the changes necessary to improve them. They grew in their relationship through commitment, communication, adjustment, and love. Often it occurred in that order. Now that you are aware of what it takes to build a good marriage, most of you can grow together before you have problems.

Several couples have told me, "I would never want to

go through this again. Yet when I see where we are now, I am glad it happened. I would never even go back to the 'glory days' of our past. Our relationship now is better than ever. But we had to pay a price to get here.''

''Will it ever be like it was?'' Go to your partner, the one you married, find the answer, and have the greatest time of your life!

Notes

CHAPTER 1
1. William H. Leach, *The Cokesbury Marriage Manual* (Nashville: Cokesbury Press, 1933), p. 31.

CHAPTER 2
1. Elisabeth Kübler-Ross, *On Death and Dying* (New York: Macmillan Co., 1969).
2. Malachi 2:16, RSV.

CHAPTER 3
1. Thomas A. Harris, M.D., *I'm OK—You're OK* (New York: Harper & Row, 1967), p. 7.
2. Leach, *The Cokesbury Marriage Manual*, pp. 25-30.
3. *Ibid.*
4. 2 Timothy 2:22.
5. Genesis 39:11,12.
6. Leach.
7. James 4:13,14.
8. 1 Corinthians 6:19,20.
9. Genesis 2:24.

CHAPTER 4
1. "Loneliness Can Kill You," *Time,* Sept. 5, 1977.
2. William Glasser, *Reality Therapy* (New York: Harper & Row, 1965), p. 9.
3. Acts 20:35.
4. Hosea 6:6.
5. 1 John 4:7.
6. Judson T. and Mary G. Landis, *Building a Successful Marriage,* Seventh Edition (New Jersey: Prentice-Hall, Inc., 1977), p. 63.
7. *Ibid.,* p. 381.

CHAPTER 5

1. Hebrews 10:14.
2. John Powell, S.J., *Why Am I Afraid To Tell You Who I Am?* (Niles: Argus Communications, 1969), p. 20.
3. Romans 3:21,22.

CHAPTER 7

1. Proverbs 15:1, KJV
2. James 1:19
3. Psalm 32:8, KJV

CHAPTER 8

1. Psalm 8:3,9, KJV.

CHAPTER 9

1. Ecclesiastes 5:10–12.
2. *Time,* July 24, 1978.
3. The *Minneapolis Star,* June 13, 1978.

CHAPTER 10

1. Hebrews 13:4.
2. 1 Corinthians 13:13.

CHAPTER 11

1. Luke 22:41.
2. Psalms 37:5.
3. Ephesians 5:21.

CHAPTER 12

1. George Ricker Berry, *Interlinear Greek-English New Testament* (Nashville: Broadman Press, 1977), p. 458 (1 Cor. 12:25–27).
2. Leontine Young, *The Fractured Family* (New York: McGraw-Hill Paperbacks, 1974), p. 140.

CHAPTER 13

1. Ephesians 5:21–33.